THE
ENDURING
ORGANIZATION

THE
ENDURING
ORGANIZATION

HOW TO
BECOME & REMAIN RELEVANT

HAL MCLEAN
FRANK MELLON

Published by Advantage, Charleston, South Carolina.
Member of Advantage Media Group.

ADVANTAGE is a registered trademark and the Advantage colophon is a trademark of Advantage Media Group, Inc.

Printed in the United States of America.

ISBN: 978-1-59932-615-3
LCCN: 2015947697

Book design by George Stevens.

This publication is designed to provide accurate and authoritative information in regard to the subject matter covered. It is sold with the understanding that the publisher is not engaged in rendering legal, accounting, or other professional services. If legal advice or other expert assistance is required, the services of a competent professional person should be sought.

Advantage Media Group is proud to be a part of the Tree Neutral® program. Tree Neutral offsets the number of trees consumed in the production and printing of this book by taking proactive steps such as planting trees in direct proportion to the number of trees used to print books. To learn more about Tree Neutral, please visit www.treeneutral.com. To learn more about Advantage's commitment to being a responsible steward of the environment, please visit www.advantagefamily.com/green

Advantage Media Group is a publisher of business, self-improvement, and professional development books and online learning. We help entrepreneurs, business leaders, and professionals share their Stories, Passion, and Knowledge to help others Learn & Grow. Do you have a manuscript or book idea that you would like us to consider for publishing? Please visit advantagefamily.com or call 1.866.775.1696.

To my wife, Barb, and my children
Jenn, Molly, and Pete.

—HAL

To my dad, who taught me to find my way, and for
little Jake as he begins his journey to find his.

—FRANK

CONTENTS

ACKNOWLEDGMENTS

I would like to thank Jesus for His direction, my family for their love, and my clients for their trust.

—Hal

I want to thank Jacque, whose constancy has allowed me the freedom to travel, work, and take the risk to build a business.

I also want to thank Clifford Ward, my first professional mentor, for showing me what persistence and clarity of thought can do. Cliff was easy to overlook at 5'6", carrying his lunch pail to work every day. He was quiet and high school educated, yet he was an innovator who helped change the oil refining industry.

Lastly, I thank my clients for their trust and for courageously leading their organizations to think in new ways.

—Frank

INTRODUCTION

L eadership is the single greatest variable in the health and success of any organization.

A company's ability to change and improve begins and ends with the leader. As that person, your role is to *ensure that your organization will endure.*

LET'S START WITH A STORY

Most of us experience a moment of enlightenment early in our careers that shapes our thinking and guides us for years. These moments often occur when we're taken out of our comfort zones and presented with new challenges and situations to which we are unaccustomed.

Hal experienced one of those formative moments shortly after graduating from college. He had just taken a job as a salesperson with a Fortune 500 company in the construction industry, and he was meeting with a general contractor to discuss insulation requirements for several construction projects. He had worked hard to get the appointment, let alone the opportunity to quote the jobs.

They had just begun when the phone rang. The contractor answered the phone and quickly told the caller "I'll be right there."

Concerned that this hard-to-pin-down appointment was about to slip away yet again, Hal looked up and asked if he needed to go. "Yes," the contractor answered.

"I hate to do this to you, but that was my superintendent calling to let me know that they're about to set the anchor bolts."

Hal asked what that meant, and the contractor explained that if the anchor bolts were set in the concrete properly, then the building would go up quickly and correctly. In his words, "Nothing is more important than getting the anchor bolts right the first time."

That was teachable moment number one for a young man new to sales and the construction world. Hal wondered, could there be other situations in which getting the anchor bolts right the first time would ensure success?

As it turns out, there are, and finding the anchor bolts that support an Enduring Organization has been the key to our success. In this book, we'll present our model of four anchor bolts for leadership, and explain how those key anchor bolts create Enduring Organizations.

Leaders must ensure that:

❋ A **relevant business model** is in place *and* the next generation business model is already in development, with recognizable triggers to begin the migration to the new business model.

❋ An **appropriate-minded leadership** team is at the helm, as opposed to a team operating with fundamental assumptions based on conditions that no longer exist.

❋ An **insightful organization** can exist, with employees at every level surrounded by information and experiences that encourage ongoing insights into the organization's performance and relationship to the industry.

❋ The company can gain real **traction for results**, going beyond the bravado of demanding cost reduction and instead embedding key elements in the organization that consistently identify high-leverage changes.

We've used these anchor bolts to improve company profits by between 50 and 300 percent in a variety of industries, including furniture manufacturing, chemical, capital equipment manufacturing, printing, and health care.

First and foremost, we are practitioners. We assess the opportunities within our clients' companies, design processes to reach new levels of performance, and personally work on-site with the leadership team until the key metrics move and are stable at new levels.

Instead of prescribing best practices and leaving when things don't work out as planned, we spend the majority of our time carrying out our projects.

If you can't understand the causes and effects of a problem with a high degree of clarity, you won't be able to design a simple and elegant solution. And if you can't find a simple and elegant solution, you won't be able to create sustainable change.

It may seem like we're oversimplifying some of the topics we discuss, but we do so with good reason.

For example, we use a very basic four-element business model, while other advisors include as many as fourteen key elements when they attempt to redesign a business model. But we've found that the more complex the model, the harder it is to execute and sustain.

Complicated solutions tend to be resource-intensive and difficult to complete. Our experience has led us to simplify—and apply rapidly.

CHAPTER 1

THE FOUR-ELEMENT
LEADERSHIP MODEL
for Enduring Organizations

A leader's purpose is to create an organization capable of providing distinctive results under varying conditions. Ultimately, leadership is the only path to an Enduring Organization.

At the center of our model is the leader's behavior—the single most important factor in becoming an Enduring Organization.

A leader achieves these results in four ways:

* By continuously *refreshing* the current business model, while drafting an early design of the next business model to keep the organization relevant.

* By *breathing* life into the organization, removing mindsets, beliefs, and assumptions that are no longer appropriate and nurturing those that are in sync with current environmental realities.

* By always *seeing* the organization for what it really is, and continuously fostering information and experiences that enable employees at all levels to have insight into how the organization really works and its relationship with environmental realities.

* By *supporting* the organization to help it gain traction in executing and sustaining high-leverage changes.

Unfortunately, we've found over the years that many leaders start by focusing on the very last element of our model, traction for results.

In their efforts to create change, they start by setting new goals for their team members instead of focusing on foundational needs like having a relevant business model and making sure that appropriate-minded leaders are in place.

These numerous, ambitious goals place unnecessary stress on the team and thus on the organization as a whole. Worse yet, the result is similar to a chronic game of Whack-a-Mole, with a new problem popping up each time one is beaten down.

If you solve problems randomly, as they arise, you'll likely end up creating more problems.

In our Leadership Model, you can see that leaders must begin
creating value by building a relevant business model, and
working counterclockwise through the Leadership Model.

Let's start with an overview of the Leadership Model.

A healthy company starts with leaders who have the appropriate perspective in each of four key areas, which comprise the
four "anchor bolts" you see at the corners of the diagram.

Counterclockwise from the starting point at the bottom left,
they are: Relevant Business Model, Appropriate-Minded Leaders,
Insightful Organizations, and Traction for Results. You'll move
through each of these pieces as you implement change in your
organization.

The first three components—the Relevant Business Model, Appropriate-Minded Leaders, and Insightful Organizations—are often invisible or overlooked, while Traction for Results is the most visible element of the model.

More accurately, many leaders are focused on only a single part of the Traction for Results anchor bolt: Goals and Metrics. More often than not, leaders who want to improve their organizations don't think about the other three elements of the Enduring Organization Leadership Model, because those areas are essentially invisible to them.

> Many leaders are blind to all but the very last step in the Leadership Model.

Many leaders believe that running the company is about staying the course, and continuing to do things the way they always have. When challenges arise, they simply do it harder and faster, focusing on the goals and metrics and wondering why they can't achieve or sustain significant results.

Frankly, leading is extremely hard work and shortcuts fail. If you really want to improve your organization, make sure that the elements of the Enduring Organization Leadership Model are in place.

It's difficult to lead well in today's environment, and we need to remind ourselves that leadership is a calling and an honor, not an entitlement.

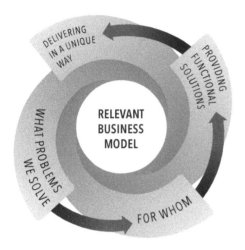

Creating a relevant business model depends on identifying the problems you solve for clients and delivering them in a unique way.

When you implement this model, start with the Relevant Business Model anchor bolt in the lower left-hand corner of the diagram. The business model is at the core of any company; it is a recipe for how the business grows and makes money.

Starting at the lower left, our model includes four components: What Problems We Solve, For Whom, Providing Functional Solutions, and Delivering in a Unique Way.

Everything in business starts with the first element in our business model, namely "What problems do we solve?"

A relevant business is not only good at understanding the problems the company is solving, but also who it's solving them *for*: hence the second element in the Relevant Business Model anchor bolt, "For Whom?"

Once the first two elements of this anchor bolt are in place, a relevant business continues by providing functional solutions to the problem, and delivering that solution in a unique way.

The company's value proposition is composed of these four elements. A value proposition is just a sentence or two that the company can take to each market segment and say, "We're able to provide a unique solution that helps your problem go away."

The goal of each of these four questions is to help your company and its products or services remain relevant. The problem is that many companies retain the same business model over long periods of time, regardless of changes in the market.

However, the business model needs to be constantly reviewed, and leaders cannot shy away from decisions about whether it should change. Most people don't consider whether their business models are still relevant; they just keep running their companies and don't ever think about doing things a different way. This is why we consider the Relevant Business Model anchor bolt to be invisible.

APPROPRIATE-MINDED LEADERS

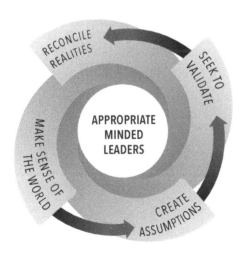

Appropriate-minded leaders must understand and work to reconcile the current realities of the world, their industries, and their businesses.

The next anchor bolt in the Enduring Organization Leadership Model is Appropriate-Minded Leaders. This is a crucial piece of the puzzle. When there's a problem with a project, it's often because the mindsets of the leaders—their assumptions and beliefs—have not kept up with the changing environmental realities around them.

When there's a problem with a project, it's often because the mind-sets of the leaders—their assumptions and beliefs—have not kept up with the environmental realities around them.

In order to have a relevant business model, you must have appropriate-minded leaders: people who understand the current realities of the world, their industries, and their businesses. As the above diagram conveys, they must be able to make sense of the world, create assumptions, seek to validate, and reconcile realities.

This anchor bolt is also considered invisible, because very few leaders are self-aware enough to examine their mindsets and realize that their assumptions and beliefs are getting in the way of business success.

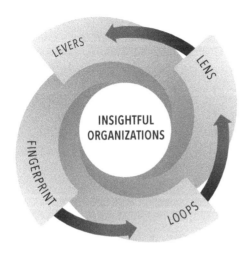

Insightful organizations cultivate opportunities for all employees to truly understand the organization and the industry.

Moving counterclockwise through the model, the next component leaders need to focus on is the Insightful Organization's anchor bolt. This is yet another key element often largely overlooked by leaders.

It is truly an insightful leader who sees the thread connecting the business model with the mindsets of the leadership and how they impact the organization.

This piece of the model is composed of fingerprints, loops, lenses, and levers.

FINGERPRINTS

A company's "fingerprint" is composed of the characteristics that make that organization what it is: in other words, what key variables make it unique?.

The fingerprint includes everything from organizational elements like problem solving and institutional knowledge to the philosophies and methodologies inherent in the organization, some of which are more effective than others.

In many ways, your company's fingerprint determines your ability to cope with environmental realities and deliver a relevant business model.

LOOPS

The next component consists of self-reinforcing cycles, or "loops." Often, when leaders attempt to change an organization, they spend a lot of time and money making those changes. However, six months later, those changes go away and the leaders are left wondering why.

Each loop represents an organizational habit that is difficult to change. Some of these loops are self-reinforcing and some are toxic, meaning that they run counter to the changes necessary to become and remain an Enduring Organization.

Many of the loops in an organization surround cultural habits, which can make them particularly difficult to see. As a leader, if you can't see the loop or understand how it's limiting your organization, then you will not be able to fracture and break that loop, and you will not be able to make significant changes.

That's how Enduring Leaders are able to make significant changes; they go in, find the toxic loops, break them, and quickly get the loop moving in a new, healthy pattern.

The trick is learning to see these loops—that's where lenses come in.

LENSES

A lens is a conceptual tool that allows you to look at your business in a different way, helping you determine how your company is performing in different areas.

For example, a lens might help you recognize that your company is operating with a made-to-order business model, yet your information systems are programmed for a made-to-stock business—so it's no wonder that you're fighting basic processes daily to conduct business.

Here's another example: Maybe your sales strategy is built on the belief that your product is fully differentiated in the market, yet your customer base has clearly decided you're undifferentiated and is only interested in talking about price. Lenses help you see which elements of your fingerprint are creating hurdles, and allow you to identify positive and negative loops so you can see what needs to change.

In short, lenses provide insight into critical pieces of your organization and help you identify the final component of the Insightful Organization anchor bolt—the levers.

LEVERS

Levers are the very few fundamental pieces of your organization that you need to target to get lasting change.

When we begin working with a company, we ask how many change efforts are in place, and we're usually told there are dozens. Under our model, we work with the leadership on two or three key change efforts—that's all.

One of our core competencies is mapping the cause and effect relationships among key variables. This process always reveals that the vast majority of problems a company is trying to solve are tied to a few key issues. These are the levers.

By drilling down into the fundamental core of the problem and resolving the lever issues, most of the other problems go away or shrink significantly. Most businesses simply don't have the resources—people, time, money, etc.—to work on a multitude of problems at once, but they do have the resources to find and resolve a critical few.

Instead of trying to fix everything at once, the leader needs to focus on finding the critical few levers within the company that will make the biggest difference.

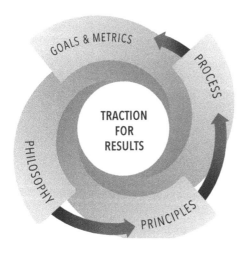

Gaining traction to create change is often a leader's only focus.

The fourth and last anchor bolt of the model, Traction for Results, is the most visible and concrete piece of the model. Because of its overt nature, it attracts more attention than any other element in the improvement process.

Traction for Results begins with the company's philosophy for how to execute change, followed by the principles that govern change efforts. The next component is the process the team will use to implement changes in a sustainable manner. Finally, goals and metrics tell us if our change efforts are delivering the results we had hoped for.

At the heart of the model are 4 key traits that
an insightful leader must possess.

To successfully put the four anchor bolts in place, the leader
must possess four key traits, which we call "refreshing," "breathing,"
"seeing," and "supporting." These four words describe both the leader's
behaviors and the impact the leader has on the organization itself.

Each of these qualities corresponds to one of the four anchor
bolts, and whatever the conditions, they help the leader create
value by staying nimble and flexible.

To get distinctive results, a leader must regularly refresh the company's business model. Relevance is the key; the leader must ensure the business model remains relevant. If the company doesn't reinvent itself, the environmental system will do it for them.

If a company doesn't reinvent itself, the environmental system will do it for them.

BREATHING

The next essential leadership trait, "breathing," involves breathing in new, fresh ideas and information and letting go of stale, outdated assumptions and beliefs.

Each of us has a "black box" that holds our beliefs, values, and assumptions—in essence, our mindset. An appropriate-minded leader must periodically reevaluate his or her black box to keep it in sync with the company's current and future business models.

Leaders need to periodically reevaluate their mindsets, or "black boxes."

SEEING

How do appropriate-minded leaders stay relevant and build insightful organizations? By continually seeing the organization in different ways, gaining invaluable new insights and creating an environment where team members are surrounded by opportunities for insight as well.

SUPPORTING

The fourth quality of a successful leader is supporting the organization as it implements key changes. Supporting means changing policies and procedures, role modeling new behaviors, and removing obstacles, all to increase the likelihood that changes will stick.

Leaders must always support their teams through the ongoing process of setting and attaining goals.

The reason most organizations struggle with change is that they start by tackling goals and metrics—the last piece of the model.

Many leaders begin, for example, by trying to cut a certain percentage of costs. The problem is that they don't create a process for achieving that goal. They have no clear philosophy or set of principles that will help them achieve that cost reduction.

These leaders are seeking to gain traction, but all they have is the goal in mind and no foundation for getting there.

Worse yet, they don't even have proof that the goal is the right one. Where is their cause and effect analysis to justify that objective?

It's a little like your tennis coach screaming "Change the score, you're losing!" The reality is that if you don't want to lose, you shouldn't focus on the score. Instead, work on your footwork, your speed, your backhand, and your strategy. Those are the levers.

Regardless of the goals, an organization's capacity to gain traction depends on a relevant business model, appropriate-minded leaders, and ability to provide insights about its current and future capability.

The basic job of the leader is to keep the company on track to become and remain an Enduring Organization. This involves being so attuned to the business that the leader recognizes when something is amiss. When conditions change and the customer base begins to drift, the leader notices the company starting to lose business it has traditionally been able to get.

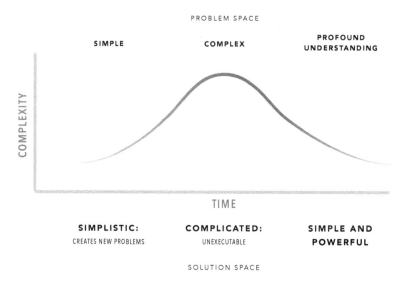

Simple solutions only work in the short term. The right
solution has to be both simple and elegant.

As you can see in the diagram above, when a problem first
arises, people tend to think it's pretty simple. Because the problem
appears to be simple, they think the solution is simple, but they're
usually missing significant information. As a result, the first
solution they try doesn't solve the problem.

Not only does that solution not last, but more often than not,
it creates new problems. This is a phenomenon we call "mowing
the dandelions."

In an hour, you can temporarily fix the problem of dandelions growing in your yard—just mow the lawn. The problem is,
you're dealing with the problem at the symptom level.

By mowing, you're sending thousands of dandelion seeds into the wind, spreading the problem into your neighbors' yards. In a few days, the dandelions will be back, and there will be more of them.

The same thing happens in organizations. People try to solve a problem at the symptom level rather than thinking it through, which ends up creating three or four more problems. Treating a symptom just delays the problem. It will show up somewhere else, like the dandelions down the block.

It's difficult to recognize cause-and-effect relationships. Often, leaders don't realize that the bigger problem was caused by the solution to the smaller problem. They get a quick result, so they think the problem is solved when it's really not.

Returning to the diagram, a closer examination of the problem space reveals that it's actually very complex. Each problem has a lot of moving parts, and at this stage you understand the complexity—or at least you think you do. You begin to execute a complicated solution, only to find that it won't work because it's so complex.

Every time you add another element to your solution, the odds of it working and becoming sustainable go down. The potential for variation in each element of the solution means that there are more things that can go wrong. Complex solutions cost more to design and implement, and they can collapse like a house of cards.

We often find this problem when we go into organizations. There are some very complicated solutions to problems, and those solutions have a lot of moving parts.

The ideal place to be when it comes to solving problems is to the far right of the diagram. This is where you find simple and elegant solutions that cut to the heart of problems with a lot fewer moving parts.

The goal is to strive to break through the complexity to come up with a simple and elegant solution, but this can be very difficult to do. In the next chapters, let's look at each element of the Enduring Organization Leadership Model in detail.

CHAPTER 2

THE RELEVANT
BUSINESS MODEL

Every business model needs to be evaluated and revised regularly.

Your role as the leader is to continually refresh and redesign your business model. This is the foundation of a successful company. By doing this, you ensure that your organization will stay relevant even as environmental conditions change.

If you're working harder and harder but feel like you're falling further and further behind, it's time to look at the foundation of your business: your business model.

Your business model is your recipe for growth and profit. When either of these variables begins to slip, it's an early warning sign that your foundation—your business model—is beginning to weaken.

Every business model has a shelf life.

A few years ago, a very sophisticated organization approached us and said that it has been implementing change efforts for the last six or seven years. While those changes had prevented decline, they had done nothing to get the company growing again or improve profits. During our assessment, it became clear that their business model was "rolling over." It was no longer connected to the environmental realities in a symbiotic way, as the model below will illustrate.

THE ORGANIZATIONAL GROWTH CURVE

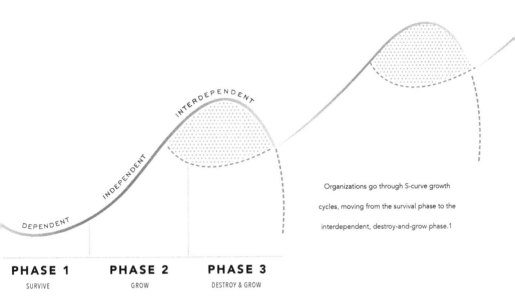

Organizations go through S-curve growth cycles, moving from the survival phase to the interdependent, destroy-and-grow phase.1

PHASE 1
SURVIVE

PHASE 2
GROW

PHASE 3
DESTROY & GROW

As you can see in the diagram, organizations start out in survival mode. They're dependent on the vision of the leader and the loyalty of their customers. That's represented in the diagram as Phase 1—the "survive" phase.

---

1 | George Land, "The Principle of Transformation", *Journal of Creative Behavior*

As they attempt to grow, most companies go through a period of trial and error. Many don't make it through this period, while others are fortunate enough to find the recipe for a product or service that stands out.

Customers have meaningful problems they want solved, and successful companies grow by finding a solution to one of those problems.

As you can see in the diagram, this is when the company starts heading up the growth curve. This is Phase 2, the "grow" phase, and it's when the company becomes a little more independent.

Now the company isn't as reliant on customers, because they're growing and they think they've got it all figured out. In this phase, the company is getting big enough to add supporting in-house services like an accounting department and customer service team. The structure becomes more complex, and silos begin to form.

But the company is beginning to ignore the market, because it's spending a lot of energy trying to figure out the complex animal called a company structure. As a result, the company starts to roll over into the next stage and performance begins to decline. This is represented in the diagram as Phase 3, the interdependent destroy-and-grow phase.

At this stage, the original business model isn't working anymore. The trick is to stretch out the Phase 2 growth by constantly improving your existing business model, while simultaneously planning the next model.

Then, when the current model shows signs of rolling over, you'll already have the framework for your next business model in place and you can start another S-curve. Ideally, this cycle should start midway between the independent and interdependent growth cycles (Phases 2 and 3).

The reason this concept is so powerful is that every company goes through these cycles. If you really think about your business, you'll find that it's somewhere on this curve.

Maybe you're at the start of a growth period. Maybe you're starting to roll over because sales are flattening out, and you're just not growing like you did five years ago. Maybe you're at the point where, if you don't make a fundamental change, you'll head into decline.

By visualizing your organization's place on the S-curve, you can begin to understand that urgency. As a leader, all your efforts to improve your current business model and plan for the future are designed to keep the company growing, whether that means increasing your revenue or refreshing your relevance. The company should always be growing. There is no neutral in an organization; you're either growing or you're dying.

There is no neutral in an organization.
You're either growing or you're dying.

In order to provide *distinctive results under varying conditions*, as we discussed in the first chapter, it's important for any business to have a business model that is current at its core.

In our model, the Relevant Business Model anchor bolt contains the four components that make up a business model:

the problems the company solves, for whom (the customer base), providing functional solutions, and delivering those solutions in a unique way.

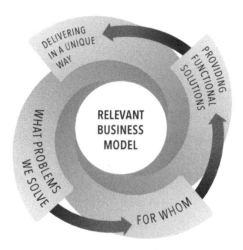

Every organization needs a four-component
business model that is current at its core.

Together, these components make up your company's value proposition, which is a sentence or two describing how the product or service solves a specific customer problem. You should write a unique, functional value proposition for each specific market segment.

The key is to remember that your company's business model must evolve with the changing marketplace; it must remain relevant. As we discussed in Chapter 1, the business model is often overlooked because leaders rarely think about its importance or relevance.

Too many companies just continue to follow the same business model year after year. They find themselves doing the same things harder and faster, instead of doing things differently—and the results are disappointing.

As we move into a deeper discussion of how leaders build enduring organizations, it's important to recognize that every piece of this model is interdependent.

THROUGH THE LENS OF FUNCTIONALITY

Finding ways your business model can evolve always starts with determining what problems your company solves and for whom.

Your business is built on problem solving. Most companies believe that they're in the business of selling a product or service, when they're really selling a solution (albeit one that happens to be embodied in a product).

If the problem you're solving changes but your product doesn't change along with it, your company will be in trouble. That's when business models begin to weaken and eventually roll over if not addressed.

That's why it's so important to think in terms of the problem your company is solving instead of the product or service you're offering—the only thing you're doing is providing a function that solves the customer's problem.

> The only thing you're doing
> is providing functionality that
> solves the customer's problem.

Customers will drop your product in a heartbeat if there's another product providing a solution of equal or higher quality at a lower cost.

Let's look through the lens of functionality for a bit. Well-run organizations understand this, and tend to do it either consciously or unconsciously.

As a business leader, the best way to keep your business healthy and growing is to adopt the mindset of being in the functional solutions business. Then, your products will ebb and flow as you layer in functionality and you won't get blindsided.

THE IMPORTANCE OF PERSPECTIVE

Earlier, we discussed how the leader must use lenses to find solutions. By looking at a problem through the lens of solutions and functions, you open up a different way of thinking and building your strategic roadmap.

For instance, let's say you're an automobile manufacturer. In the functional solutions diagram on the next page, you'll see the levels of functionality your products could offer as solutions to customer problems. This trajectory suggests not only what your next step should be, but where your industry is likely heading... the driverless car.

In recent years, we've seen automobile functionality evolve to include radar cruise control, automatic braking for unseen objects, automatic parallel parking, and rear-view cameras. These are all layers of functionality developed to solve customer problems as environmental conditions changed.

FUNCTIONAL SOLUTIONS | EXAMPLE: SELF DRIVING CARS

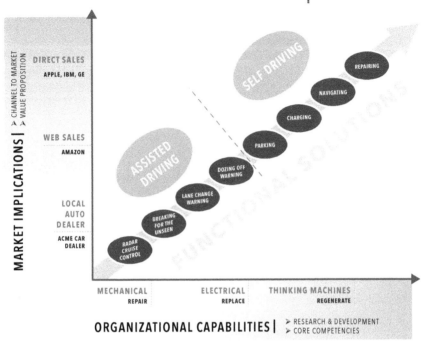

Strong leaders are open to using different ways of
thinking, or lenses, to find the right solution.

The functional solutions diagram helps us to remember that
functionality is central to solving relevant problems. As the set of
problems in an industry evolves, a company's portfolio of functionality must also evolve to stay in sync with the market and
anticipate as-yet-undiscovered customer needs.

As the need for new functionality progresses, there are two
primary areas of impact: the market implications (e.g. channel
and value proposition per market segment) and the capabilities
the organization must possess (e.g. research and development and
core competencies) to deliver a differentiated value proposition.

In our example, you can see that as the functionality evolves, the channel to market may well evolve with it, ranging from purchasing a car at the neighborhood dealer to ordering directly from the producer.

The organization's R&D agenda and core competencies must also enable the evolution of the technology from mechanical to electrical to (potentially) an intuitive orientation that learns, adjusts, and repairs itself.

The purpose of this illustration is not to debate the future of the auto industry, but to offer a critical thinking tool—a lens—for your business. Experiment with this model as you undergo your corporate or product line strategic planning. Start by asking what portfolio of problems (including those that the customer has not yet connected with your industry) could you be solving? What is the best functionality to apply to these problems, and in what general sequence?

The one thing we'd like you to take away from this section is that if you think about your products in terms of different functions, you'll maintain focus on solving people's problems. This is the functional solutions lens.

It's not about the product; it's about the functional solution.

As you layer on different functionalities, you must go to the market differently, and you need different technology and capabilities. When you develop a functional solutions road map, you begin to prepare your market strategy as well as the organizational capability you need to deliver that functionality. *This is a tremendously important North Star around which to align your improvement efforts.*

One of the most common reasons companies enter decline is that they're seeing the world through the lens of their products. The customers, in contrast, look at things through the lens of their problems. Never forget: the only thing sacred to the customer is a functional solution…not your product.

THE BUSINESS MODEL SHELF LIFE

First IBM dominated, then Microsoft, and now Apple. Every business model has a shelf life, and they're more like milk than wine—often souring before you realize they're out of date.

All business models will eventually "roll over." For example, bookstores, record stores, and video rental stores that were successful for decades have all been upended by the digital world.

Earlier in the chapter, we introduced the idea of initiating a new S-curve midway between the growth and destroy-and-grow cycles.

This helps your company avoid rolling over on the S-curve and getting too far into a downward cycle.

THREE HORIZONS

HORIZON III
THE DAY AFTER
TOMORROW

HORIZON II
TOMORROW

HORIZON I
TODAY

To stay relevant, you need to always have a second model underway.

As we said earlier, every business model has a shelf life. In order to stay relevant, you always need to have a second business model in the works.

This is demonstrated by the Three Horizon Model, as described in the book *The Alchemy of Growth: Practical Insights for Building the Enduring Enterprise*, by thought leader Mehrdad Baghai, Stephen Coley, and David White. In this model, the intersection of the lines represents the launching of the next model, and business leaders should already have the next model on deck before they reach that intersection.

This next business model should be in the works while the business is growing and the first business model is still on the incline. If you wait for the signs that your business model is rolling over, you're far, far too late.

Elite athletes will tell you, "If you wait to drink water until you're thirsty, it's too late" (because you're already dehydrated). Likewise, if you wait until your business model is rolling over, it's too late—you're already outdated.

Elite athletes will tell you, "If you wait to drink water until you're thirsty, it's too late" (because you're already dehydrated).

In the Three Horizons Model, the first horizon represents the current business model. Leaders who continue to plan for only this business model will be caught off guard, because the model will eventually peak and roll over, leaving them scrambling.

By the time they wake up, it's very difficult to put new capabilities in place fast enough to implement a new business model. Your degrees of freedom are limited when you're on the defensive in the marketplace.

The second horizon is the business model the company will advance to next. While the company is still operating in Horizon I, its leaders should already be formulating and preparing to launch Horizon II. They should already have the Horizon II business model ready, allowing the leaders to make resource and strategic decisions about where the company is going.

Even while the company is in the first horizon, it's possible to begin thinking about Horizon III, the "day after tomorrow" business model. For example, in the automotive business, this means acknowledging that driverless cars are in the future, and beginning to plan for that. It's very likely that one day, we're going to get in our cars and program them to drive us to work while we busy ourselves with other matters. You might as well plan for it now.

THREE HORIZONS STRATEGIC FRAMEWORK:
ONE POSSIBLE FUTURE OF HEALTHCARE

		Horizon I: Optimize Current Model	Horizon II: Build New Business Model	Horizon III: Broadly Embed New Business Model
Business Model		Mechanical	Mechanical and organic	Organic
Strategy		Plan & Push	Predict & Pull	Respond in real time
DELIVERY	WHO	MD & PA	RN & technician	Technician & yourself
	WHAT	–	–	–
	WHERE	Hospital, office, clinic	Clinic, retail, "minnie mills"	Workplace, home, remote
	WHEN	Into illness	At beginning of illness	Before illness happens
	DEGREES OF FREEDOM	High	Moderate to low	Low to none
Physician's Role		Independent, uncoordinated (hospital, other MDs)	Interdependent, coordinated (hospital, other MDs)	"Watson" smarter, community wellness
Charges		Complicated, cost plus, high variation (individual treatment)	Simple, value-based, moderate variation (individual treatment)	Simple, value-based, low variation (community prevention)
Scaling Solutions		One hospital at a time	Multiple hospitals and clinics at a time	All delivery channels in real time
Revenue Stream		100% healthcare treatment	75% health care treatment, 25% value-added solutions (tools, tests, pathways, etc.)	50% health care treatment, 50% value added prevention solutions (tools, tests, fitness, information, pathways, etc.)
Language		Procedures & services	Functionality & capabilities	Digital & statistical
Key Capabilities		• Leadership engine • Scaling process • Functions re-purposed	• "Watson" • Partnerships	• Organic, morphing, self-responding organizational structure • Continual migration of value down the value chain
Priority & Resource Development		80% time/leadership resources	15% time/leadership resources	5% time/leadership resources

In an evolving market, changing the key components of
your business model can set you up to succeed.

The Three Horizons Strategic Framework table on the previous page explores one potential future of the healthcare system. As you can see, industry changes (whatever they turn out to be) will leave some health care organizations throughout the value chain at a disadvantage, while others will have a distinct advantage.

As you read over our incomplete example framework for the healthcare industry, you can see how strategic conversations can help you ask the appropriate questions and set a path forward through a changing landscape. Caution; this is merely an illustration to show how the model can be used. We are not providing a pathway forward for the healthcare industry but merely an incomplete tool to demonstrate how it can be a used for strategic discussions and eventually decisions.

If you pretend our illustration is somewhat accurate, you can see the questions it prompts and the key decisions that must be made over the next five to seven years in this industry.

Take a look at the row labeled "Physician's Role" in the left-hand column. In the current business model, Horizon I, physicians have typically been independent, but that's changing.

Their private practices haven't been working so well, and hospitals are buying up these practices to add more doctors.

If these independent physicians don't get absorbed by hospitals, they're often combining into practices of five or more just to survive. Either way, they're searching for a new business model to remain independent.

Though many try to fight it, physicians are shifting from an independent role into an interdependent one. They're being forced to become coordinated, both in the hospital and in the larger practices.

To get you thinking about the future, we've also thrown in the example of Watson, the intuitive IBM supercomputer. Many of the facts that physicians are trying to keep in their heads right now, along with millions of statistics, medical records, and other variables, are soon going to be managed by supercomputers. These supercomputers are able to make predictions based on individual patient data that physicians could never have come up with, in spite of their decades of experience.

The entire medical world is going to change. The physician of 10–15 years from now will not look like the physician we see today.

We're also seeing a shift in the revenue stream. The current model is that the physician treats patients and then gets paid different prices for the same services based on a range of variables. Potential legislation could shift that pricing structure significantly, yet the physician still has to deliver the same services.

Like healthcare, your industry is changing. And as with the lone private practice doctor of the 1950s, your business model has a shelf life.

It's not automatically bad news to have to redesign your business model. It can be very exciting and energizing when done proactively. Should you choose to wait too long, your organization will be limited by decline, big cost cuts, big layoffs, and shareholder and board pressures, resulting in less and less freedom to act.

You've heard us say again and again that a leader's job is to ensure that the company's business model remains relevant, but it goes beyond that. The appropriate-minded leader is one who says, "I like my business model, but I know I'm going to have to break it one day."

Remember…

❊ Blend the four components of the business model:

- the problems the company solves,
- for whom (the customer base),
- providing *functional* solutions,
- in a differentiated way,

  …thus leading to a value proposition for each key market segment you serve.

❊ Look through the lens of functionality.

❊ Start the design of your next business model before you need it.

❊ Draft a functional solutions road map, and let it drive your channel/customer and your technology/capabilities decisions.

❊ Utilize the Three Horizons Model to ensure you'll have the next-generation business model ready when environmental realities dictate a change.

While it's absolutely necessary to have a relevant business model, it alone is not sufficient to build a healthy organization. Appropriate-minded leaders are the next essential element.

These are people who understand that the company's business model has a shelf life. They know they need to be spending a certain percentage of their time working on the next business model, and they're making an effort to ensure that their fundamental assumptions about the business environment sync up with the new business model. Let's take a look into our "black boxes" together ...

CHAPTER 3

APPROPRIATE-
MINDED LEADERS

Y ou now have a plan to refresh your current business model, and the framework of your next business model is in place to stimulate profitable growth at the right time. To quote thought leader Eli Goldradt, "That is necessary but not sufficient."

Your role is to *breathe* in new, appropriate beliefs and values and breathe out old assumptions that no longer reflect your current reality. The leader's job is to ensure that the rest of the leadership team is able to do the same thing—breathe. This enables an appropriate-minded leadership team to lead effectively and ensures a *relevant* organization.

A few years ago, we worked with an organization to design and implement a new business model. They hadn't had any growth for six to seven years, and the leaders were smart enough to know the "rollover" was eminent.

We gathered the best and brightest, and the CEO charged our team with this goal: design and implement a new business model that will produce at least 10–12 years of double digit profitable growth. Our only boundary conditions were to not drift from the company's key core competencies or code of conduct.

We did exactly that. It was one of the hardest, most rewarding engagements we've ever had the honor to work on.

At the meeting to describe the new business model, the CEO asked two questions. First, he asked what the probability was of this new business model giving them double-digit profitable growth for the next 10–12 years. We answered that there was an 80 percent probability. Then, he asked what the probability was of the new model being successfully implemented. We answered that there was a 50 percent probability of successful implementation.

He took a deep breath and asked, "Under what conditions could we change that to 80–90 percent chance of successful implementation?" We paused and said that a number of his key executives were too invested in old mindsets that were closely tied to the old business model, and that they would not sufficiently embrace the new business model.

He privately asked for the names of these leaders with unbending mindsets, and promised to have appropriate-minded leaders in place shortly.

He then returned to the team and gave the go-ahead to implement the model as planned. The right leaders were in place shortly, and the company went on to double its size and triple its profits.

One of our favorite quotes from the great management expert Peter Drucker is, "The greatest danger in times of turbulence is not the turbulence; it is to act with yesterday's logic."

Leaders often do this unknowingly.

As we mentioned earlier, having appropriate-minded leaders is a crucial piece of the puzzle. Problems that arise are often the result of leaders who have not kept up with the environmental realities.

Often, a leader started or joined the business 10, 20, or 30 years ago. The company became successful because the way the business was structured was appropriate for the time.

But the world changes, businesses ebb and flow, and our mindsets and assumptions may not stay in sync with the environmental realities. So regardless of a company's past success, what matters is that today's leaders think differently than the leaders of the past. They must prioritize differently, and their decision-making must be different.

Appropriate-minded leaders who are aligned with the new relevant business model are an essential ingredient in the recipe for success.

You've done the very difficult job of redesigning the business model, but if you launch it with leaders whose assumptions are still tied to old environmental conditions, it won't work. If you're not willing to do the courageous work of aligning the leadership with the new business model, prepare to fail.

If you're not willing to do the courageous work of aligning the leadership with the new business model, prepare to fail.

In Chapter 2, we briefly discussed the importance of leaders having their "black box" assumptions in sync or aligned with the new business model.

The beliefs, values, and assumptions that comprise your mindset—or "black box"—must be aligned with the environmental and organizational realities.

The black box is our metaphor for a leader's mindset, foundational assumptions, values, and core beliefs. Everybody has a black box.

Let's navigate the diagram counterclockwise, starting with "Make Sense of the World." When we find something that helps us make sense of the world, we move from seeing if it works, to believing that it will work consistently, and finally to knowing that it is just plain true for us. This core assumption is now in the black box.

Over time, these foundational assumptions can become stale, and leaders often forget to re-examine them to see if they are still appropriate.

Because core beliefs drive so many day-to-day decisions, we forget to stop and examine them in the shifting contexts of our lives. Also, people have a tendency to unconsciously surround themselves with other people and information that validate their core assumptions.

Soon, we begin to notice that our assumptions are not ringing quite as true as they once did, and we have to choose to reconcile the environmental realities with our foundational assumptions.

This point is where we choose to turn back or learn, grow, and change. This breathing out of old, outdated assumptions and breathing in of new, appropriate assumptions is a critical capability for leaders who want their organizations to endure.

When something works repeatedly over time, you assume it's "true" rather than simply functional. The more frequently an assumption is validated, the more it slips from your conscious mind into your subconscious mind. You don't think about it anymore. It doesn't occupy any conscious time or energy.

The effect is that you're using these assumptions to make sense out of the world without consciously thinking about it. Remember Dr. Drucker: "The greatest danger in times of turbulence is not the turbulence; it is to act with yesterday's logic."

Yesterday's logic was appropriate in the past under certain conditions. But today, it is a different context—a different world. Has your mindset, the contents of your black box, remained in sync with those environmental realities? If you're not careful, your black box can become aligned with a world that no longer exists, causing you to act with yesterday's logic.

> "The greatest danger in times of turbulence is not the turbulence; it is to act with yesterday's logic."
>
> PETER DRUCKER

For example, you may believe that you're a specialty solutions company, and so your strategies, systems, and skills are all aligned with that assumption. But what if that's no longer the case for a certain segment of the business? Operating with the belief that you're a specialty company when a portion of your business is now a commodity will create a significant disconnect with your processes, products, and markets.

This can happen in any number of key areas. Did your company begin as a made-to-order business, but has migrated over time to a made-to-stock business model, or vice versa? Has the value proposition in the value chain moved, and you haven't recognized it? If any of these migrations have occurred, your business model needs to shift. In order to retool the organization's strategy, systems, and skills, the leader's mindset has to change.

FOUR LEVELS OF CHANGE

DEPTH OF THOUGHT AND ACTION

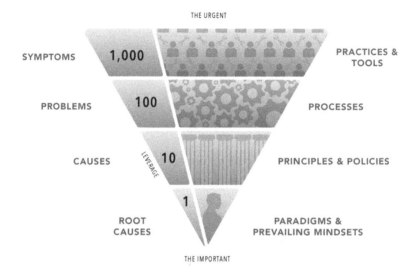

In this model, the mindsets of the leadership team hold a fundamental position at the bottom of the model, directly influencing everything above.

In the Depth of Thought and Action diagram, your "black box" full of assumptions, values, and core beliefs is positioned at the very bottom of the model (Paradigms & Prevailing Mindsets). From that foundational location, it drives everything you do and affects how your organization operates.

Each level of thinking involved in creating change is listed down the left side of the model: symptoms, problems, causes, and root causes. Whether you're trying to resolve an issue with a weekend project or redesign a complex organizational issue, these four layers need to be addressed if you want to find a simple, elegant solution.

Most people try to resolve issues or create change at the symptom level because they want to get things done as fast as possible and spend as few resources as they can. But in the end, that's kind of like mowing dandelions that will grow back with a vengeance. When you create more problems by trying to address the symptoms, it's often because you don't understand what's going on.

Let's look again at the Depth of Thought and Action model. Next to the depths of thought listed down the left side are the numbers 1, 10, 100 and 1,000. These numbers aren't a formula or algorithm; they're just for illustration purposes. They represent the exponential number of resolutions you can potentially get at each depth.

For instance, let's say you find ten causes for your core issue. If you fix those ten, 100 problems will be resolved, and probably 1,000 symptoms will disappear.

When we work with an organization, we dig down deep to find the root causes and end up working on only two or three issues. We go straight for the bottom of the model, where the troll—the root cause of an issue—is lurking.

For example, let's say you've taken a day off. It's a gorgeous morning, and you're sitting by the river reading your favorite book. All of a sudden, you hear screaming and splashing—it's a swimmer struggling in the water. You jump in and grab him, pull him to the bank, and make sure he's okay. Before long, he's off on his merry way.

Within the hour, it happens again. You're sitting there reading when, all of a sudden, another person comes along splashing and shouting for help. You get her out of the water and off she goes.

This happens several times before you decide you've had enough of these interruptions, and you set off to find the cause.

Traipsing through the woods along the bank of the river, you don't know where you're going, what you're looking for, or what you're going to do when you find it.

Eventually, you see a bridge. From your vantage point on the bank, you can see a troll hiding underneath the bridge, guarding it. You watch an unsuspecting man approach the bridge and, just as he reaches it, you see the troll reaches up to grab him and throw him in the river.

The troll is the cause of all the people splashing around in the river. It will require a little more work to get rid of the troll than to rescue a swimmer, but once you do, you'll be able to enjoy your day off in peace.

Why are people so hesitant to seek out causes? Is it because they don't know where they're going? Because they have to stop doing something enjoyable? Because they don't know what they'll find? Maybe they're afraid that what they'll find is much bigger than they are.

People have the tendency to operate at the symptom level, where they can be the heroes. In the diagram, this is the top portion of the model, where everything seems urgent. It's intoxicating to be the hero who pulls drowning swimmers from the river, and that makes it much harder to stop what you're doing and decide to find the root cause.

It's not as intoxicating to look for the troll. The odds are you might not find him, and even if you do, he might be bigger and tougher than you. But unless you try, you'll be forced to spend all your time rescuing swimmers.

Here's the lesson of our fable: if what you're doing isn't solving the problem, find a bigger problem to solve.

If what you're doing isn't
solving the problem, find a
bigger problem to solve.

Solving problems at the symptom level where everything seems urgent is like playing whack-a-mole—you whack one mole back down into his hole, and two more pop up like the arcade game.

Typically, when people try to resolve issues or create change within an organization, they tackle the components that are listed down the right-hand side of the Depth of Thought and Action model: practices and tools, processes, principles and policies, and paradigms and prevailing mindsets.

As you can see, practices and tools are at the surface where everything seems urgent These are usually the first things people tackle when they see a symptom.

Processes are deeper and more fundamental. People often turn to processes when the symptom is determined to be a real problem, and changing a few tools and practices isn't working.

Digging down a layer further, you find principles and policies. These are even more fundamental, and are often examined as the leadership searches for a cause.

However, the most powerful piece of this diagram is at the very bottom. The element that drives everything and has the power to make problems and symptoms go away is the paradigms and prevailing mindsets of the leadership—essentially, the leader's "black box."

The prevailing mindsets of the leadership drive all the principles and policies in an organization, which in turn drive the processes, which then drive the practices and the tools.

The root cause of most problems in an organization is that the leader's mindset needs to shift. A change in the governing paradigm of the business makes all the difference.

The root cause of most problems in an organization is that the leader's assumption base (black box) needs to shift.

COMPARING MINDSETS: AMERICAN AUTO MANUFACTURER VS. JAPANESE AUTO MANUFACTURER

A number of years ago, an American auto company was looking for ways to bring new car models to market faster with fewer defects. At that time, it took five or six years to commercialize a new car from concept to customer. It was impossible for them to predict what the customer was going to want that far in advance, and history had proven that by the time they released a new model, the tastes, needs, and wants of the market had shifted.

So the company leadership changed its assumption base and decided to get new models to market faster. They needed to be able to design, build, and debug the new vehicles not in five or six years, but in two.

At that particular time, the American company was partnered with a Japanese automobile manufacturer. The vice president of operations for the American company got together with his counterparts at the Japanese company, and for two days they tossed around ideas about how the American company could commercialize faster.

But after two days, the American company's vice president realized that even if he could magically implement everything the Japanese team suggested, he still wouldn't be able to get cars to market in two years. He stopped and asked his Japanese colleagues, "What are we missing?"

After discussing the question amongst themselves, they came back and the Japanese team leader drew a diagram of the American automotive manufacturer's approach to the process of commercializing a new car. We've recreated it for you below.

In the diagram, you'll see the number of problems represented by the vertical axis, and time represented by the horizontal axis. The date of the new model car coming off the line is represented by a point and line extending up from the Time axis.

MINDSETS REGARDING PROBLEMS

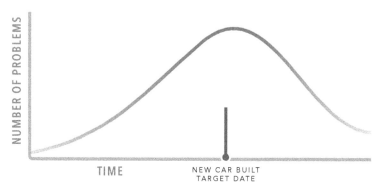

AMERICAN AUTOMOTIVE MANUFACTURER'S MINDSET
➤ THERE IS AN INFINITE NUMBER OF PROBLEMS
➤ PROBLEMS ARE BAD; AVOID THEM AS LONG AS YOU CAN

NUMBER OF PROBLEMS

TIME

NEW CAR BUILT
TARGET DATE

This model illustrates that the American company fundamentally believed that an infinite number of problems could arise during the process of designing and building a new car. Those problems, they assumed, were bad. As a result, they avoided them for as long as possible. They didn't want to hear about the problems; they just wanted to get results.

The result was the curve you see in the diagram. The area underneath the curve represents the number of problems the American team found as they got further and further in the process of commercializing a new car. Notice that the number of problems increase as the new car gets closer to its launch date, and that many of the problems are still not resolved when the car hits the market.

Then, the team from the Japanese manufacturer drew another diagram, this time illustrating their attitude toward problems. They explained that they believe that there is a finite number of problems to be resolved in any project, and that early-found problems are treasures.

The Japanese company actually rewarded employees for finding problems early. Conversely, the culture at the American company—questioning people about why a problem exists—only served to intimidate employees and drive problems underground, to be revealed in the ninth inning when they could no longer be hidden.

Being associated with a problem in the American company could result in punishment. At the Japanese company, people were celebrated for bringing problems to light as quickly as possible.

MINDSETS REGARDING PROBLEMS

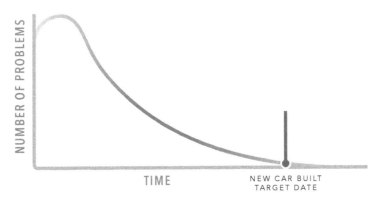

JAPANESE AUTOMOTIVE MANUFACTURER'S MINDSET
➤ THERE IS A FINITE NUMBER OF PROBLEMS
➤ EARLY FOUND PROBLEMS ARE TREASURE

NUMBER OF PROBLEMS

TIME

NEW CAR BUILT
TARGET DATE

When a car company finds a problem with a new model early, it can often take care of the issue with a few keystrokes on the computer. Finding the problem, a year or two later could require a significant redesign.

That's a powerful example of how a paradigm shift in the leader's mindset can make all the difference.

The health of any company depends on a relevant business model that facilitates growth. However, you'll never be able to put one relevant business model in place and have another waiting on deck unless you've got appropriate-minded leaders who are ready for the upcoming business model.

At the beginning of this chapter, there was a story about a company that couldn't implement a new business model without installing appropriate-minded leaders in key positions.

A leader who creates value is always looking for new ways to see the company.

A leader who creates value is always looking for new ways to see the company. The leaders who were removed from those positions weren't going to make the necessary mindset shifts. They weren't going to go into their black boxes and do the heavy lifting that needed to be done to remove outdated assumptions and beliefs. They had to be replaced with people who already had mindsets that would serve the new business model, or who would be willing to adopt a new mindset.

When you encounter new information that you believe to be true, you add it to your black box, where it becomes a part of the beliefs, values, and assumptions that make up your mindset.

If those beliefs, values, and assumptions linger in the black box for too long, they can become toxic. Occasionally, you have to "breathe out" old, stale beliefs, values, and assumptions, and breathe in fresh ones.

Because it requires substantial self-awareness, it's very difficult for most leaders to continually refresh their mindsets. The leaders who regularly breathe in new information to replace old beliefs are the ones you want in your organization.

In working with so many leaders across all kinds of companies, we've observed a number of core beliefs that these people often hold in common. We'll end this chapter with two of the most powerful.

1. OPTIMIZE THE WHOLE ORGANIZATION INSTEAD OF MAXIMIZING THE PIECES

To add value to their organizations, leaders need to get comfortable embracing what often seems counterintuitive.

For example, we often hear leaders talk about maximize each individual element of their organizations. But when employees are forced into goal-driven situations and every department is attempting to maximize its variables, the organization just doesn't function very well.

To create a healthy organization, leaders must optimize the whole, not maximize the pieces.

The key is to shift your mindset from maximizing the pieces of the organization to optimizing the organization as a whole. Everything in a business is interdependent, so if your goal is to improve productivity and profitability, it's a little more complex than turning all the dials up to 10.

In some departments, operating at the fastest possible rate has negative impacts on other departments and the organization as a whole—imagine perishable goods piling up more quickly than they could be packaged and shipped.

Organizations today must be seen as Rubik's Cubes. Make a move to align two yellow squares, and you may be disturbing a block of six blue squares somewhere else.

A classic illustration of this principle is balancing sales, R&D, and operations. If you maximize sales, you can overwhelm operations capacity and leave no time for R&D to validate new products for manufacturability. That's a problem that will hobble your long-term relevance.

It's so much easier to have common goals for improvement. It's fair this way; all departments get treated the same and are working together toward the same goals. You just need to do the hard work of modeling out the organization's collective targets to find the "sweet spot" in each department that serves your overall goal of optimizing the organization.

2. CONFIDENT, YET UNCERTAIN

Most people's confidence rests on their certainty of being able to do something they have done in the past. In their black boxes, they have an assumption that confidence equals certainty. However, this belief becomes toxic when you're faced with totally new situations.

When your tried-and-true business model starts to break, you'll have to do new and different things very rapidly and you won't be able to draw on your past successes for confidence.

But confidence is absolutely essential to your ability to lead change in your organization. The source of your confidence needs to shift from past successes to the skills that will help you solve the right problems going forward.

We call this attitude "confident, yet uncertain": uncertain about how it will all unfold, yet confident that we will figure it out.

This subtle shift frees the leaders and the performers to rapidly try new things, learn, and adjust until they're successful.

A mindset that allows you to be confident only when you're certain of the outcome will:

❈ Freeze you in the current state.

❈ Make you expect to get new changes perfect the first time.

❈ Block innovation.

❈ Delay, if not prevent, the examination of old "black box" assumptions that must be "breathed out."

When you redesign a business model, there's a lot of innovation, as well as trial and error. Your mindset needs to be able to shift rapidly, and you need to be able to make adjustments based on what's working and what isn't. You don't need to be certain; your confidence as a leader comes from knowing that you have all the skills you need to figure it out.

Remember:

- ❈ The new business model will not get implemented without appropriate-minded leaders whose "black boxes" are in sync with the new business model.

- ❈ Leaders must learn the skill of "breathing": exhaling old mindsets that are out of sync with the environmental realities, and inhaling fresh beliefs, values, and assumptions.

- ❈ We all need to muster up the courage to examine our black boxes and admit that some of what's in there, though once appropriate, is no longer serving our needs and goals.

CHAPTER 4

INSIGHTFUL
ORGANIZATIONS—
FINGERPRINTS

In the next few chapters, we'll explore the tools a leader can use to see the organization with a high degree of clarity, and provide information and experiences that give all performers insight into how the organization really works.

FINGERPRINTS

The leader's role is to create an environment that continually offers fresh information and experiences that provide insight for the entire organization.

Here are some of these insights:

* "This product line has slowly morphed into a commodity product line, yet our pricing and customer support still reflect a specialty product strategy. No wonder our costs are rising and our sales are declining!"

* "Our business model is made-to-order, yet our computer systems and workflow processes are designed for made-to-stock. No wonder it feels like running up a sand dune to make and ship our products!"

❋ "Our order-to-ship cycle is 40 days, but it could be two days. If we redesigned our processes to be more efficient, we could ship twice as many orders in half the time."

It is the role of the leadership to create an environment that allows these kinds of insights to pop up regularly. One such way to do that is by using the tools of an insightful organization, which we call fingerprints, loops, lenses, and levers.

The next few chapters are about using these tools to assess where your organization is and gain real insight so that instead of having dozens of change initiatives, you can work on a critical few that will provide real, focused results.

An Enduring Organization must have a relevant business model and appropriate-minded leaders, but though necessary, these alone aren't sufficient for organizational health. You must also have an organization that's capable of implementing the new business model and that reflects the appropriate mindsets. That is the Insightful Organization, the next anchor bolt of the Enduring Organization Leadership Model.

The tools and models you'll see in the next few chapters are designed to help you do an "MRI" of your organization. You can use them to discover which facets of the organization will support the changes you need to make, and which facets will work against the changes.

There is a direct correlation between the contents of the leader's black box and the cultural norms in the organization. Make no mistake, leaders—you are the culture carriers. If you like your company culture, pat yourself on the back. If you don't, it's your responsibility to change it.

Your organization's fingerprint is the unique set of qualities that makes it what it is.

For example, let's say there are around a dozen key elements that help define how any organization operates. Determining which of these will be most effective in creating change reveals a lot about an organization.

Regardless of how complex an organization is, there are 10 or 12 key elements of a company's culture that control performance.

In the Organizational Set Point diagram below, you'll see each of these elements—leadership, strategy, functions, cost control, problem solving, organizational improvement, information, operations, quality, and relationships—placed on a continuum. On each line, the far left represents an unhealthy, low-performing organization, and the far right represents an insightful, high-performing organization.

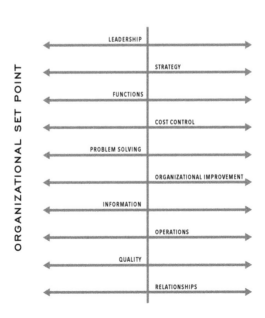

If you want to be an insightful, high-performing organization that can implement a solid business model with appropriate-minded leaders, you need to be working your way from left to right on each continuum. Now, let's take a closer look at several of these elements of culture individually.

LEADERSHIP

From Command & Control	To Service & Support
• *Administrators/bureaucrats* • *Gatekeepers* • *Creators of rules and regulations*	• *Leaders* • *Barrier removers* • *Principles to work by*
Fundamental Leadership Assumption *"Since we are the source of truth, we will need to use rules and regulations to ensure the performers do what we say."* *"We have the right kind of leaders, and we just need to do the same things harder and faster."*	*Fundamental Leadership Assumption* *"Our job is to create the environment so that the performer can win. The source of truth will always be a combination of executive leadership and the performers."* *"We will need to infuse our leadership with a mix of different-minded leaders."*

When it comes to leadership, there are "Command and Control" leaders, and there are "Service and Support" leaders.

Command and Control leaders are those who behave like administrators, bureaucrats, and gatekeepers. They create rules, regulations, and policies. They say things like, "Don't do anything until you check with me" and "I'll make the final decision."

In their black boxes, these leaders carry fundamental assumptions like "Since I'm the source of knowledge, I need to use rules and regulations to ensure that my employees do what I say."

They also believe that the right kind of leaders are already in place, so all they need to do to fix problems is continue to do the same things harder and faster.

Conversely, the leadership in an insightful, high-performing organization is composed of barrier removers who create principles to work by.

For instance, instead of acting as gatekeepers, the insightful company's leaders remove barriers. Instead of creating rules and regulations, they create a handful of guiding principles to work by so that employees feel trusted and empowered to do what they need to do.

STRATEGY

From Reacting & Copying	To Responding & Inventing
• *Too many, ever-changing "shiny balls" from consultants* • *Chasing after someone else's "best practices" to copy* • Maximizing *the* pieces *of the organization*	• *A fundamental redesign of the business model* • *Inventing our own solutions rapidly* • Optimizing *the* whole *organization* • *Installing the capabilities that will enable the organization to create differentiated sustainable results under varying future scenarios.*
Fundamental Leadership Assumption *"We do not have the answers in house, so we must be led by outside entities that we believe do have the answers."*	*Fundamental Leadership Assumption* *"We will create the environment of rapid reduction to practice and innovate our way to solutions that work in our organizations."*

Far too often, strategy becomes a hybrid of best practices, fads, and playing out organizational momentum, instead of what it should be: a differentiated value proposition and roadmap of core competencies robust enough to get distinctive results under varying conditions.

Far too often, strategy becomes a hybrid of best practices, fads, and playing out organizational momentum, instead of what it should be: a differentiated value proposition and roadmap of core competencies robust enough to get distinctive results under varying conditions.

Best practices are not fully transportable, because every organization has a different capability profile. The best practices that thrive in one environment don't necessarily transfer to another; everything is different, from the leadership to the strategy, processes, core competencies and cultural norms.

There are tools and techniques broad enough to work in many cases, but it's not safe to assume that they will all work for your organization. As with all of the essential organizational elements, it will be the leader's mindset that is the key driver.

From Uncoordinated Self-Maximizing	To Coordinated Organization- Wide Optimizing
• *Maximizing functions/silos* • *Acting in isolation to other functions* • *Self-proclaimed holders of "truth"* • *Gatekeepers of decisions and the pace at which decisions are made* • *We are entitled to the work*	• *Optimizing the whole organization* • *Ongoing, coordinated process with other functions* • *Blending function's and operation's knowledge for balanced solutions* • *Respond to organization's needs at their pace of doing business* • *Functions will compete with outside contractors for the business*
Fundamental Leadership Assumption *"We are the source of truth, not the line organization, therefore we must control decisions and their pace."*	*Fundamental Leadership Assumption* *"We will coordinate with the other functions in order to deliver support to the line organization at the speed dictated by the pace of the marketplace. All the while keeping in mind we are to optimize the whole organization."*

Understanding the purpose and role of the functions in the organization is critical-these are the finance, human resources, legal, quality, etc.

It's worth your effort to do a little critical thinking about the functions that support your business. Are they the source of a strategic advantage? Do they seem to operate in isolation, or are they well integrated with other functions? Are they designed to be self-reinforcing, or do they set out to serve the line organization?

When you have uncoordinated functions all fighting to have their requests and expectations met simultaneously through the line organization, expect to provide less value to the marketplace.

When you have uncoordinated functions all fighting to have their requests and expectations met simultaneously through the line organization, expect to provide less value to the marketplace.

It's a different story when you have all the functions coordinated at the executive level, with their demands balanced throughout the year. Learn to identify the purpose and strategic nature of your functions, and keep them serving the needs of of the line organization that rely on them. If that isn't possible, contract that function out to someone who can.

COST CONTROL

From Cutting People Events	To Improving Processes Continually

• *Cut people*
• *Reduce capability*
• *Incremental cost savings*
• *Compliant culture—*
  "playing not to lose"
	• *Improve processes*
	• *Increase capability*
	• *Order of magnitude of cost savings*
	• *Committed and innovative*
	  culture—"playing to win"

Fundamental Leadership Assumption *"We can cost-cut our way to success."* *"The fastest way to cutting costs is to have real hard savings by cutting people now".*	*Fundamental Leadership Assumption* *"No organization has ever cost-cut their way to success. They have cost-cut themselves out of business."* *"The most appropriate way to significantly lower costs is to continually create and flow more value year over year."*

At times, it becomes necessary to outplace people. But continually improving processes is certainly preferable to episodic staff reductions that don't have the intended effect. A consistent focus on process improvement can lessen the frequency and magnitude of layoffs.

When cost control becomes particularly troublesome, the first place to look is your business model. Is it weakening and losing value? If so, how much and how fast? Is the main issue price erosion, market share loss, weak new product commercialization backlog in R&D, or something else? Checking the health of the business model can help you see when layoffs alone will not solve the problem.

Cost cutting is always more concrete and immediate than doing the heavy lifting of assessing and upgrading your business model. However, cost cutting can be a slippery slope. Leaders usually put it off until the viable options have narrowed and reflexive actions are necessary.

First, many leaders start with the "Let's be fair to all" approach, where horizontal cuts are applied to every department at the same level. When that doesn't solve the problem, they attempt a deeper cut across all areas.

Soon, the organization reaches the point where more cuts would place quality, safety, and the brand's reputation at unacceptable risk levels.

Then, the focus shifts from horizontal to vertical cuts—the closing of a function, department, plant, product line, etc. The organization eliminates capabilities and/or markets. Far from signaling that our people just need to work harder and faster, vertical cost cutting is symptomatic of a weakening business model.

The best cost control we know is to continually provide higher-value solutions with ever-increasing throughput through the same asset base year over year.

The best cost control we know is to continually provide higher-value solutions with ever-increasing throughput through the same asset base year over year.

From Temporary "Band-Aid"	To Permanent Solution
• *Focal element: People* • *Problem list: "101 issues long"* • *Time: No time for analysis* • *Depth: Symptom level* • *Solution Duration: Short* • *Organizational Impact: Creates more problems and feeds same old problems to return. "Whack a Mole"*	• *Focal element: Process* • *Problem list: 3-5* • *Time: Make time for analysis* • *Depth: Root cause, with system implications* • *Solution Duration: Permanent* • *Organizational Impact: Permanent solutions which then pull in the next set of appropriate problems to solve*
Fundamental Leadership Assumption *"We do not have the time or people…so, put a Band-Aid on it and get back to work."*	*Fundamental Leadership Assumption* *"We will make the time and people available to find a lasting fix because this is our work."*

An organization's methods of problem solving can be a strong indicator about the company's health and the leadership's mindset. Problem solving goes on everywhere, all day long, and how it's addressed affects what we call the Holy Grail of measures: throughput, cost, and quality.

Let's get this clear—you'll never be free from problems. Solving them is the nature of the work. The trick is to always be tackling the *right set of* problems. When you solve problems effectively, you earn the right to solve the next set of problems, which should be more compelling, complex, and challenging.

When you solve problems
effectively, you earn the right to
solve the next set of problems,
which should be more compelling,
complex, and challenging.

If you're continually faced with the same set of problems but are unable to see permanent fixes, you'll find yourself stuck playing whack-a-mole—the same problems popping up over and over again.

Success is facing a more difficult portfolio of problems each year, because you're finding permanent solutions for lesser problems and taking on higher-leverage issues as you go.

From Maximizing the Pieces	To Optimizing the Whole
• *Unit of Focus: The individual units* • *Make every unit max out on its metrics* • *Change Portfolio: Large* • *Resource Deployment: Few resources spread over far too many problems with insufficient critical mass to solve the issue*	• *Unit of Focus: The whole organization* • *Help each unit understand its role to optimize the whole organization* • *Change Portfolio: Critical few* • *Resource Deployment: Moderate resources spread over critical few problems with enough critical mass to solve the issue*
Fundamental Leadership Assumption *"If we break the organization down into its pieces and then maximize each unit and then add them all up together, we will have a maximized organization."*	*Fundamental Leadership Assumption* *"The organization is a dynamic interconnected system. We will find the appropriate points of leverage in the organization and balance the optimizing and suboptimizing of the various elements of the organization in order to optimize the whole."*

While organizational improvement is a close cousin of problem solving, it has a different goal. Instead of focusing on solving a specific problem, the target of organizational improvement is the underlying philosophy that governs the portfolio of problems to be solved.

A leader should be focused on problems that represent the system dynamics of continual improvement in all areas, plus specific high-leverage improvements in a few well-understood and well-chosen areas.

Frankly, the common belief that you should "maximize all areas as much as you can" speaks to a leadership team with more bravado than profound understanding of how the organization works. Trying to amp up performance in every area throws organizational capabilities out of sync, producing a number of unintended consequences. If you plan significant performance improvements, be sure to model out the implications of each change and you'll end up with fewer surprises.

INFORMATION

From Compliance & Policing	To Insight & Continual Improvement
• *Purpose: Accountability* • *Structure: Closed* • *Flow direction: Pushed out by organization's needs*	• *Purpose: Insight leading to continual improvement leading to competitive advantage* • *Structure: Closed & Open* • *Flow direction: Pulled from performer's needs*
Fundamental Leadership Assumption *"Information is used to manage risk and to hold people accountable."*	*Fundamental Leadership Assumption* *"Information must be converted to insight to create a learning organization that provides continual improvement and competitive advantage."*

The need for reports, audit controls, and performance metrics is real, but the need relates more to providing insight at the performer level than to holding people accountable.

Accountability is important, but what's more essential is that the information that flows throughout the company truly provides insight for each performer and a more fundamental understanding of how the organization works as a whole.

While working on a project some years ago, we asked one of our clients a series of questions about the overall health of the business.

Not getting sufficient answers, we asked the executive team to bring all their reports to the conference room and hang them on the wall.

Then, we asked them to select the ones that were relied upon by the most people and believe to be the most accurate. As it turned out, few of the executive teams actually used them, and those that did lost faith in the reports once we began to ask questions about the process of gathering the information.

The takeaway is that often, the information the performers receive is just noise, rather than a signal that can be used to improve the organization.

OPERATIONS

From To-Do Lists	To Predictable Capability
• *Inside people's head* • *Experts in the "what"* • *Focus on the "what"*	• *Visible* • *Learners in* how *to make the* what *go better* • *Focus on the process and the content*
Fundamental Leadership Assumption *"We are experts, who just do it. This is just the way it is in our industry."*	*Fundamental Leadership Assumption* *"We are learners, who install and continually improve process capability."*

Operations must be a series of interdependent processes connected by predictable outcomes.

Some organizations treat their work as a series of transactions and to-do lists, with the real expertise hidden inside John or Jane's head. Smaller organizations fall prey to this more often, yet even in larger organizations, there are pockets where expertise isn't shared and processes lack predictability, making it difficult to plan accurately. Instead, every organization's experts must pour their knowledge into the process and ensure that organizational IQ is not lost.

QUALITY

From Conceal	To Reveal
• *Cost* • *Periodic, reactionary events* • *Owners: Quality and risk groups* • *Risk: Conceal to lower*	• *Investment* • *Continual proactive* *process improvement* • *Owners: Everyone* • *Risk: Reveal to lower*
Fundamental Leadership Assumption *"Control quality by concealing mistakes in the quality and risk groups."*	*Fundamental Leadership Assumption* *"Improve quality by revealing mistakes throughout the organization for learning and implementing permanent solutions."*

The fastest path to higher quality is simple: reveal rather than conceal problems. This fundamental belief must be instilled in all performers in the organization. As we discussed in Chapter 3, early-found problems are treasures, and should be treated as such.

As Brian Joiner points out, leaders who demand unrealistic performance improvements without a solid process set themselves up for failure. Such demands will result in members of the organization gaming the metrics to comply with a demanding leader, robbing the organization of the chance to truly improve the business. Sadly, these leaders often create cultures of fear and compliance, with little to no effective problem solving.

RELATIONSHIPS

From Independent	To Interdependent

• *Comfort: Commonality*
• *Units: Individuals*
• *Leverage: Department*
• *Metrics and goals:*
  Individual units
	• *Comfort: Diversity*
	• *Units: Teams*
	• *Leverage: Interface between functions*
	• *Metrics and goals: Flow*
	  of value across units

Fundamental Leadership Assumption	*Fundamental Leadership Assumption*
"We can do this ourselves, *within our department."*	*"We will need to work across functions* *and outside the organization."*

As each organizational set point so far has highlighted, all elements of an organization are connected in a single system, and each must do its part to understand how its actions affect the other elements in the system.

High-leverage changes are those that impact elements of the business far beyond their immediate area. Many times, leverage is found at the interface between functions, customers, and suppliers. Taking the time to consider and understand the implications for all stakeholders before you make a change will produce higher levels of commitment and effectiveness.

THE ORGANIZATIONAL SET POINT

An organizational set point is a bit like your body's core temperature. Part of the human body's functionality is that it creates heat by burning food, while perspiration cools us off. The two systems are working at the same time, balancing each other out at roughly 98.6 degrees Fahrenheit, or the human body's "set point."

Likewise, your organization's fingerprint is composed of performance in each of the key elements we've discussed in this chapter. Your job as the leader is to assess what needs to move where, and start moving it.

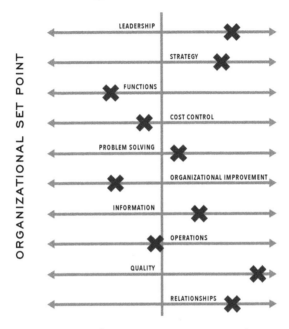

Your organization's fingerprint, or organizational set point, is composed of where you fall along each of these continuums.

As the leader of your company, if you were to be brutally honest with yourself and put an "X" on each line representing where your company stands with each of these characteristics, you would be able to determine your organization's set point, or fingerprint.

Just like the human body, in a business there can be two forces constantly vying for control. For example, within the leadership, there may a faction pushing for a "Command and Control" style of leadership, and another faction pushing for a "Service and Support" model.

The forces are rarely equal in an organization, so the set point won't likely be neutral. One force is pushing harder than the other, but which one is it? Is it a healthy or toxic influence?

CHAPTER 5

INSIGHTFUL ORGANIZATIONS— LOOPS

I n the last chapter, we discussed how the leader's beliefs influence and create the company's fingerprint, as well as how to determine your organizational set points.

Now let's talk about loops—the self-reinforcing patterns of behavior that characterize how the organization performs on an everyday basis.

LOOPS

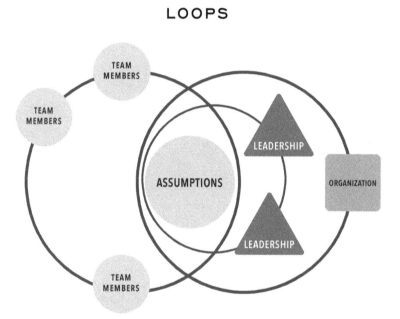

All day long, patterns repeat themselves—governing how employees are hired and fired, what happens when key performance targets aren't met, how the company handles low (and high) performers, how crises are managed, and much more.

These loops are ingrained in the organization and are typically quite difficult to break. At the heart of each organizational loop is an invisible, foundational assumption that was set in motion years ago by leadership.

Here's an example. One organization we worked with does their planning in the fall, defining their business plan for the coming year. January rolls around, and the loop is set in motion: Set the targets. Conceal problems. Prepare to fail and blame.

We experienced this loop with one of our clients, and were struck by how unbending the plan was as it got implemented. We tried our best to influence the client to make real-time adjustments, to no avail. Though the original plan had many unintended consequences, no attempt to learn and adjust was made.

After careful research, we uncovered the centerpiece of this toxic loop. The foundational assumption was, "We hold our people accountable. If they say they're going to do something, then they'd better damn well deliver or be dealt with accordingly." The leadership's mindset was *hold people accountable at all costs.*

This toxic loop is driven by the leadership's assumption that they should hold people accountable at all costs.

Contrast that toxic loop with one that looks like this: Set targets, see what's working and what isn't, make adjustments, and prepare for success and celebration.

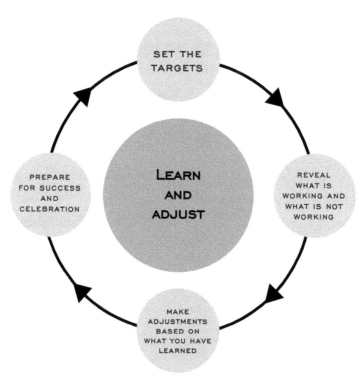

SET THE
TARGETS

LEARN
AND
ADJUST

PREPARE
FOR SUCCESS
AND
CELEBRATION

REVEAL
WHAT IS
WORKING AND
WHAT IS NOT
WORKING

MAKE
ADJUSTMENTS
BASED ON
WHAT YOU HAVE
LEARNED

This growth loop is driven by the leadership's assumption
that adjustments are healthy and necessary.

The leadership mindset at the center of this growth loop would look something like this: *It's too complex a world to lock a plan in place and not make adjustments as we implement. I will hold you accountable for rapidly learning and adjusting; I will hold you accountable for a target set six to nine months ago but not the how to reach that target.*

Self-reinforcing loops are what make an organization's fingerprint quite stable. This is demonstrated by the diagram below.

In the center of this diagram are the leadership's assumptions. Their mindsets are embedded in the organization by how they communicate, the way they prioritize, the way they source solutions, and by what they choose to reinforce.

THE LOOPS DIAGRAM

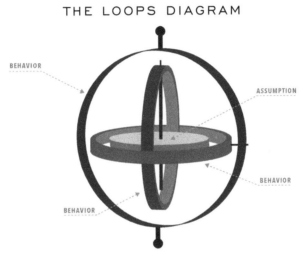

Once the leadership's core assumptions are embedded in the organization, it's very difficult to break their momentum. This is true of growth loops as well as toxic loops.

As the diagram illustrates, the behaviors revolving around the leader's assumptions act like a gyroscope, holding the key assumptions in place.

The leaders plant seeds daily based on their beliefs, and they share their assumptions through role modeling and other behaviors that influence team members. In time, the team starts to absorb and perpetuate the leadership's mindset. Their behavior is consistent with the leaders' assumptions, and soon the organization's behavior is as well.

There are two kinds of loops. There are toxic loops that are not effective, don't get good results, and suck energy out of an organization. Toxic loops stem from mindsets that are controlling and unchanging, disconnected to the environmental realities and they bring an organization down.

Then there are *growth* loops. They're effective, they get good results, and they breathe life into an organization. Growth loops stem from mindsets that are current and relevant, and they help an organization grow.

Whether the loops are toxic or growth-oriented, they reinforce the leaders' assumptions and make them very hard to change.

For example, we were once working with a printing company that had lost several major clients and was now losing hundreds of thousands of dollars every month. The company had two plants: a flagship facility that was operating at capacity, and a smaller plant that was still serving a few clients.

The company had purchased a new printing press to install at its flagship plant, and planned to close the smaller plant once the new press was up and running. Here's the catch: the new press at the flagship plant wouldn't be up and running for another seven months.

We looked at the situation and told the leaders that we could open up enough capacity in the flagship plant that they would be able to close the smaller plant. Moreover, we told them we could do this in two months, and we did—a 30 percent capacity increase at a constrained plant in 59 days.

How did we do it? By breaking a key loop caused by the leader's mindset.

We started with an analysis of the numbers. We found a chart of the product defects that had occurred per run, day, shift, week, and month. At a certain point, all of the defects stopped abruptly.

How did this happen? Just prior to the drop off, the CEO had sent out an email that said, "I will no longer tolerate any quality defects in this organization." So, everybody just stopped recording them. The defects were still there, but the team members were afraid to report them.

This is an example of an organization caught in a toxic loop. The leader's assumption was that quality defects were a problem, so he refused to tolerate them. As a result, every other leader in the plant stop reporting defects, rendering the data inaccurate and useless.

That's how the leadership ends up reinforcing a bad assumption. When the values and beliefs in the leader's black box aren't appropriate, he or she spreads a toxic mindset throughout the company culture and quality is affected.

We had promised to free up at least 30 percent more capacity in the flagship plant, and much of that capacity was being lost to product defects and change overs.

Once the systems to find and report defects had been reestablished, we were able to quickly and systematically identify and solve the bigger problems, freeing up capacity and meeting our goals.

How do you break toxic loops? The best way is for the leader to role model growth loops instead. If there are bad habits in the organization, it's because the leaders have bad habits.

The leader's behavior reinforces his or her core assumptions, and the people who report to the leader role model that behavior as well. Just as with a powerful gyroscope, it's very difficult to change the central axis—the leader's black box—once it's set in motion.

By now, you realize you can't pull off a good business model without an appropriate-minded leadership team. As the leader, your words, actions, and decisions are the manifestations of what's in your black box. Everyone in the organization is watching and learning. They're going to follow you, the leader, and carry what they learn throughout the organization.

CHAPTER 6

INSIGHTFUL ORGANIZATIONS— LENSES

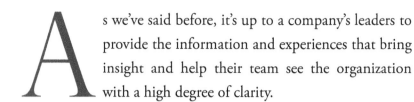

s we've said before, it's up to a company's leaders to provide the information and experiences that bring insight and help their team see the organization with a high degree of clarity.

This is accomplished by looking through the appropriate lenses. As a leader, you've got to learn to see the pieces of your organization like you've never seen them before.

Here's an example. We worked with one company where the leaders thought that, because it took so long to get an order processed, they must certainly be capacity-constrained. They assumed the company was slammed with work.

We went in, watched the operations for a while, looked over the data, and said, "You're probably operating at a third of your available capacity." They replied, "No way." After a few weeks of working together, the vice president of research and development told us, "I didn't know we had more capacity until you came and told us we did." That's the power of looking at your business through a different lens.

To create an Enduring Organization, leaders need to be able to see the business in ways many people can't, and consistently bring fresh insights to the team.

For that vice president, discovering that his organization had hidden capacity was an important insight. It was a real win for him because the R&D needed machine time in order to develop and test new products for manufacturability. If the plant was operating at full capacity and just barely getting orders out the door to customers, there was no way he could develop new products, but we were able to show him how he could get time on the machines.

A lens is simply a way to look at your business from a different perspective in the hope of gaining some insight.

The diagram below represents the classic specialty versus commodity product lens.

SPECIALTY VERSUS COMMODITY

The market's goal is to commoditize your specialty products as quickly as possible. You fight this as well as you can by maintaining a differentiated value proposition, but over time, this differentiation erodes.

The market is the sole entity that determines a product's specialty or commodity status. More often than not, this shift comes well before the product's creator is aware of the change. The company is left providing an undifferentiated commodity product at a specialty price, and they're surprised when sales volume and market share decline.

You can use this lens to plot the specialty or commodity status of your various product lines three years ago, today, and three years from now, and create strategies to maintain your differentiated position.

MAXIMIZE VERSUS OPTIMIZE

PROBLEM SOLVING

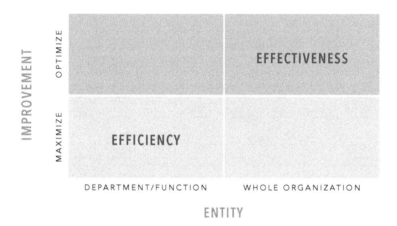

A lens provides a way to juxtapose different factors or priorities, as you can see in the above diagram representing how organizations think about problem solving. In this particular case, the horizontal axis represents the entity you're trying to improve (either a department, a function, or the whole organization), while the vertical axis represents your approach to improvement (maximize or optimize).

Most leaders assume that if they set goals to maximize all the company's departments or functions, they're asking every department or function to work at its very best. The problem is that maximizing in this manner doesn't take into account the impact each change has on the rest of the organization.

In contrast, optimizing means working toward the best outcome for the organization as a whole, finding trade-offs that take the implications of each change into account.

Systems dynamics in organizations suggests that if you maximize every department individually, you'll end up with a suboptimal organization. You have to balance things out; optimization means getting the right mix of key variables throughout the entire organization. Most organizations that want to maximize just put the pedal to the metal, but that doesn't work.

Think about your body. What if your brain sent a message to your body that said, "Okay, on three, I want every system to maximize itself?" You would be catatonic. Some of your organs and other body parts need to be suboptimal for others to be optimized. There has to be give and take to find the sweet spot.

Let's look at another lens that offers insight. The dynamics that are felt throughout the organization play out different purposes inside an organization.

FUNCTIONS

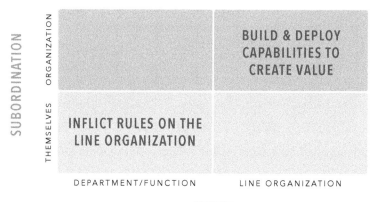

Imagine Pinocchio with six or eight strings pulling him in different directions throughout the day. He'd look spastic, wouldn't he?

The above diagram represents two totally different paradigms governing the role of the functions in an organization.

One paradigm suggests that the functions optimize themselves as they see fit independently of the rest of the organization.

The other paradigm optimizes the company as a whole by coordinating selective change efforts across the organization throughout the year.

For example, if the company is in manufacturing, the limiting factor is probably demand levels on the production line. In addition to balancing demand on the line, this paradigm treats functions as responsive supports that must move at the speed of the line organization—not the other way around.

We've worked with several clients where supporting functions were limiting the speed of production—"Still waiting on legal to approve the contract," or "still waiting on IT to provide the following results," or "still waiting on Human Resources to source good candidates," etc.

The leader's job is to use the lens to enable insight.

There are countless lenses for examining your business. Invent your own! The purpose is insight into the real nature of the organization and what needs to change. If you build a lens and it offers no insight or critical conversations, drop it and create another.

THE PROCESS OF THE LENS

The leader's job is to create a lens by juxtaposing certain variables. When we ask the leaders of an organization to whom they are subordinating, themselves or the entity, and then ask whether they are optimizing or maximizing, it helps them see their business in ways they've never seen before. That's the goal for the leader: to use the lens to provide a different perspective and create insight for the organization.

Leaders who are able to view their organizations from a different perspective are often able to shift their black box assumptions and realize that their agenda, priorities, and goals need to change—learning to see what has not been seen before.

Through fingerprints, loops, lenses, and levers—the latter of which we'll discuss in the next chapter—leaders can begin to see things they've never seen before. They understand how to breathe out some of the toxic carbon dioxide of old mind-sets that are no longer appropriate and breathe in new mind-sets and assumptions that are more appropriate to the current environment.

The leader's job is to see the organization in ways that aren't normally seen. His job is also to create an environment in the organization so that performers have insight about how the organization works and doesn't work and how it needs to evolve to stay connected with the environmental realities.

He's able to understand how to align the business model so that it's relevant, helping the business to grow and make money. But this is only accomplished with appropriate-minded leaders who can support the business model and an insightful organization that ebbs and flows and makes the necessary changes to be able to win, interact, and implement the new business model.

CHAPTER 7

INSIGHTFUL
ORGANIZATIONS—
LEVERS

Before we move on to the Traction for Results chapters, there's one more very important step. To create lasting change, you must find *the differences that make the difference.*

These differences, which we call levers, are the critical few things that move an organization one way or another. Instead of working on dozens of different change efforts that can't all be effective and may even work against each other, choose the two or three fundamental things that will raise the water level of the harbor, not just fix a leaky boat or two.

As we've said before, when mindsets shift, they can change everything. Here's a powerful example of that.

We were at a plant, meeting with leaders from the same company that had decreed that there be no more quality defects in their products. It was a very controlled and autocratic company culture in which employees had learned to hide problems. By all appearances, there were no more quality defects.

We were discussing problem solving, and suggested that the leaders' black boxes needed to change. We asked, "What's the mental shift that has to occur with you folks? You're the culture carriers, and change isn't going to happen out there on the plant floor until the mindset in here shifts."

One employee, who rarely spoke, leaped out of his seat and said, "We've got to shift our mindset from concealing problems to revealing problems. Find them fast, reveal them, and fix them."

That realization was life changing for him. The next day, he went out and removed anything on the manufacturing floor that could hide or conceal a problem.

A couple of days later, a great many problems had been discovered as a result. For instance, moving boxes away from the line had revealed that one of the production lines, which had always been stop-and-go, had a bad bearing that was leaking fluid. He had also removed the doors from storage cabinets, solving another common problem—supplies running out before anyone realized they were low.

When you shift from concealing to revealing, your whole world changes. You can reorient your mindset around detecting, fixing, and preventing problems. The focus on revealing instead of concealing is how you find the few critical levers that will make a big difference.

You may have a hundred problems that you're trying to solve, but in reality, those problems are caused by two or three critical levers. If you move the needle on those, you'll improve or eliminate many or most of your problems.

RAISE THE WATER, DON'T TRY TO FIX EACH BOAT

Rather than trying to fix the boats in the marina one at a time so that each is riding a little higher in the water, we try to figure out how to raise the water level.

In other words, we don't maximize the pieces of an organization. We optimize the entire organization.

A few years ago, the leader of a hospital brought us in to look at a problem with the emergency room, which serves as the gateway to the hospital. The majority of patients admitted to the hospital came through the ER. He wanted to shorten the wait time in the ER to give the hospital a competitive edge, because the big differentiator in the area was how long it took a patient to be seen.

Since this was our first experience with a hospital, the leader wanted us to start with the smallest ER in the system. However, the real problem was that costs were rising faster than the hospital was being reimbursed, and if they didn't make a change soon, profitability would be negatively affected. Knowing that, the last place we'd want to start was the smallest hospital. We needed to begin with the system's largest hospital, which provided the majority of the system's profits.

We also knew that we could figure out how to shorten the wait time in the ER. We'd have to start inside the hospital itself, which wouldn't in its current state be able to absorb the increased flow from a maximized emergency room. Our goal was to create a vacuum in the hospital that would pull patients out of the ER faster.

This is an example of maximizing a piece of the organization instead of optimizing the whole organization. The leader wanted to maximize the ER. We wanted to optimize the whole organization.

CAUSE & EFFECT MAP | IMPROVING HOSPITAL PROFITABILITY

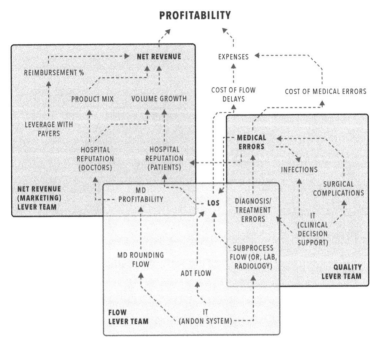

A cause-and-effect model helps identify the critical few levers.

The diagram above is an example of how to discover the levers in your organization. Be very careful not to force too much detail into your analysis, or it can inadvertently mask the signal with a bunch of noise.

As you can see from the top of the diagram, the goal is profitability. What are the critical things that affect profitability? Net revenue: that's the good stuff, that's cash coming in. But then there are the rising expenses.

A multitude of things impact expenses and revenue, but what are the one or two things—three at the most—that have the biggest impact?

The way we discover levers is to bring in team members from within the organization, and then we start walking down the causal tree to discover the clusters of factors that impact the critical few levers.

We don't just perform a few brainstorming sessions; we ask process questions that really force people to think, like "Your life depends on improving revenue. If you can only choose two things to change, what are they?" Along the way, we stop to validate information and adjust the numbers with the goal of refining our analysis and creating financial models and measurements to test our improvement strategies.

In the cause and effect map for improving hospital profitability, there are three components we chose to work on: net revenue, medical errors, and length of stay (LOS). For each of these components, we asked ourselves, "How are we going to improve in these areas?"

Ultimately, we deduced that by shortening the length of stay (LOS) from five days, when a patient was only supposed to be in the hospital for three, we would be able to get patients in and out faster and decrease medical errors. The statistics are pretty clear that for each day in the hospital, a patient is exposed to more opportunities for mistakes, infections, and other complications, so patient outcomes would likely be better as well.

With shorter lengths of stay, instead of running 20 patients through a unit in a week, we might be able to get 30 through safely and with a high standard of care. If the average stay is five days in that unit and we can get it down to three, what happens to the opportunity for medical errors? It goes down.

The lever in this example is the length of stay. We started by working on the most complex floor in the hospital—a nursing unit—because it was causing 80 percent of the extended stays. We asked the chief financial officer to model the numbers, and his figures revealed that if we achieved our goals, profits would reach levels the hospital had never seen before. "It's impossible," they told us.

We applied the 80/20 rule and presumed that most of the problems in the organization were being caused by just a few causes. No matter what else came along, we refused to chase the issues causing 20 percent of the problems in the hospital. We just kept after that one nursing unit, because it was causing 80 percent of the problems. That unit was a key lever.

LEVERS LEAD TO GREAT RESULTS

We didn't understand everything about the hospital business, but we understood cause and effect, physics, and system dynamics, so we worked with the hospital staff to figure out the solutions.

Even though we were asked to visit other facilities, we refused, because the majority of the system's sales were in that one hospital, and *we never want to be more than an arm's length away from the true levers.*

You never want to be more
than an arm's length away
from the true levers.

Again, all of this is achieved by first identifying the levers. Depending on the complexity of the problems to solve and how quickly we have to move, we'll often use a statistical model as well as a cause-and-effect tree to illustrate the problem and identify levers.

In this case, we were able to show that if we moved one thing by 20 percent, it might start to move another variable by 60 percent. We didn't need to touch everything on the cause-and-effect tree, we just needed to find those critical few levers. Once you shift those levers, a lot of problems will resolve themselves.

For instance, when we took the average stay from five and a half days to just under three days, quality naturally came along for the ride. The number of infections dropped dramatically, even though we didn't target those infections. In those two-plus days that we trimmed off of the average stay, we were able to admit another patient. In essence, the hospital was able to treat two patients in about the same amount of time that it used to treat one, with better patient outcomes.

For us, increasing profitability isn't about cutting staff. We rarely cut—that's going after the wrong levers. As the organization improves it's thoughput, in this case patients, through the same asset base, the costs naturally go down. The hospital is able to deliver more care to more people and the physicians are able to treat more patients and patients get home faster with better outcomes...a win, win, win.

Instead, we improve the throughput, which in this instance means treating twice as many patients in the same amount of time and making twice the money, with costs and quality coming along for the ride.

Throughput is *always* a lever.

When any organization is able to improve its overall throughput, it directly influences the "Holy Grail" of metrics—throughput, quality, and cost. We all want the throughput to increase, quality to go up, and costs to go down. The dynamics of the three measures are such that when throughput goes up, quality has a natural tendency to go up, and costs have a natural tendency to go down. Though it seems counterintuitive to some, as throughput improves, quality goes up. Often, people assume that moving faster will cause them to make more mistakes; in fact, you won't be moving faster per se. Instead of doing the same things harder and faster, you're doing things altogether differently, and that's a game changer. We tell our clients that when they're moving levers in the right direction, their world will turn Technicolor.

LEVERAGING, LIVING THE LEVERS

There's a story that's often told about the CEO of a fast food chain who decided that the levers in his business were the food and the wrappers.

As people lined up at the door of his office with problem after problem to discuss, the CEO made it very clear that if they were here to talk about improving the food or improving the wrapper, he would listen. Otherwise, he had no time.

That leader was spending his valuable time where it counted, and nowhere else.

Years ago, a similar situation arose in the airline industry. Arriving and departing fights were late, customer satisfaction was dropping, and so on. The chairman of one of the airlines decided that the critical variable was on-time departures. Once people were in the air, they would get to their destination, but getting them airborne was the challenge.

For the next year, he focused on on-time departures (his lever) and spent his time monitoring aircraft departures via a special computer installed at his desk. If he saw that a flight was not moving on time, he'd get patched in to the cockpit and ask the pilot why the flight hadn't left yet. He didn't have to do that many times, because news of what he was doing spread like wildfire. Suddenly, everyone in the industry was hunting for their company's levers and aligning their activities around them.

Southwest Airlines discovered that their lever was turn-arounds. Southwest learned that when a plane is stationary, the company is not making money, so their focus was on turning each plane around as fast as possibly.

They also use only one model of airplane, the Boeing 737, all of which have the same dashboard. Why? Because they understand that similarity and standardization is a lever in their business. Instead of having dozens of types of planes that pilots must be certified on and other crew members have to work around, they've just got one. Training is simplified. Maintenance is simplified.

Southwest isolated the levers in their business to keep their planes flying, rather than sitting on the tarmac.

The leader's job is not only to identify levers, but also to create an environment in the organization where the team members can see the levers and focus their work around them. Then, when new levers arise, the team will be prepared to recognize them and share their insights with the leadership.

We are all teed up to move on to the Traction for Results chapters, and this is where organizations go from being *insightful* to truly *enduring*—can they actually implement high-leverage changes? Many a new, relevant business model has been left on the cutting-room floor because of the company's inability to execute.

CHAPTER 8

TRACTION
FOR RESULTS—
PHILOSOPHY

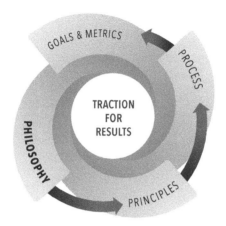

Y ou may remember that in Chapter 1, we discussed how the first three components of the Enduring Organization Leadership Model—Relevant Business Model, Appropriate-Minded Leaders, and Insightful Organizations—are often invisible or overlooked by corporate leaders, while Traction for Results is more visible and tangible.

Specifically, most leaders are focused on only a single part of the Traction for Results anchor bolt: goals and metrics. However, they are doing themselves and their companies a disservice by ignoring the other elements that build traction for results: Philosophy, Principles, and Process.

Let's talk first about how organizations can cultivate a company philosophy that works.

Years ago, we were meeting with the top executive of an organization that is now $50 billion in size to talk about the key issues facing him. He listed several, but lingered on how to determine what to work on and what not to work on. He had a tremendous resource base and could apply it to almost anything, but he struggled with finding the differences that truly make a difference. Of equal importance, he and the organization needed to learn to say no to lower-level changes.

The leader's job is to provide support when the organization is undergoing change efforts. This support consists of changing policies, providing resources, setting priorities, and encouraging the organization to experiment and rapidly learn and adjust. As the leader does that, the organization begins to gain traction for results when implementing change. The leader provides the support—the organization gets the traction.

As we said at the beginning of the chapter, the first component of Traction for Results is having a philosophy that works.

Toyota has a philosophy: "We build the people, they build the cars." By pouring resources into its people, Toyota makes them better critical thinkers and disciplined problem solvers. The company gives its employees the tools and the techniques they need to do their jobs better, and creates a culture and environment that fosters innovation and ideas. Then, the cars almost take care of themselves.

That's a pretty distinctive philosophy.

If you want to create the kind of environment that gets results, start with a good philosophical foundation.

Unlike Toyota, most organizations operate with a philosophy that holds people accountable and beats them up when things don't turn out as expected. In other words, you have to get it right on the very first try.

Wilbur Wright once said:

"Now, there are two ways of learning to ride a fractious horse: One is to get on him and learn by actual practice how each motion and trick may be best met; the other is to sit on a fence and watch the beast a while and then retire to the house and at leisure figure out the best way of overcoming his jumps and kicks. The latter system is the safest, but the former, on the whole, turns out the larger proportion of good riders. It is very much the same in learning to ride a flying machine; if you are looking for perfect safety, you will do well to sit on a fence and watch the birds; but if you really wish to learn, you must mount a machine and become acquainted with its tricks by actual trial.[2]"

We subscribe to Wilbur's philosophy. The basis of our success is helping clients get very clear on the levers in their businesses. It usually takes a while to identify the levers in an organization, but as soon as we find them, we put the lessons into practice right away. We get on that fractious horse and ride it. That's our philosophy.

The story of the invention of the airplane is a fascinating look at how innovation takes place. The Wright brothers, two bicycle makers, were up against the Smithsonian Institution with all of its science, cash, and resources as well as many efforts in Europe.

The chart below illustrates the differences between the Wright brothers' flying machine and the "aerodrome" of Samuel Pierpont Langley, the secretary of the Smithsonian Institution, who led the government's efforts to be the first in flight.

2 | From the book *To Conquer the Air*, James Tobin.

Approach	Langley's aerodrome	Wright's flyer
Key problem to be solved	*Power and speed (powerful, light engine)*	*Stability and control*
Required conditions	*Calm air*	*Normal (gusty) wind conditions*
Design	*Design the final version of the manned aerodrome at the outset*	*Make hundreds of changes to the design along the way, based on results of experiments*
Testing	*Test an unmanned 1/4 scale model once, just prior to the maiden voyage of the full-scale aerodrome*	*Immediately reduce concepts to practical tests, often within a day*
Theory & measurement	*Assume theory is well-established*	*Challenge theory when careful measurements and test results reveal discrepancies*
Failure	*"Failure is not an option": success on the first try is the only desirable result*	*Failures often surface new critical issue; solving those leads to ultimate success*
Project management	*Delegate key tasks and manage from a distance*	*Hands-on design and testing*
Number of flights	*None*	*Hundreds*
Resources	*Budget nearly $70,000 (after cost overruns). Full access to the resources of the Smithsonian Institute*	*Spending under $1,000. Use available resources in the bicycle shop*

The different philosophical approaches to flight.

Langley and the Wright brothers represent two fundamentally different philosophies to innovation and getting results.

The Smithsonian group kept trying to put more horsepower into Langley's machine, thinking that enough power would overcome many problems. Meanwhile, the Wright brothers were after stability and control. The Langley team thought that flight could only be achieved in calm air; the Wright brothers realized a flying machine would be useless if it couldn't handle difficult condition winds, so they headed to North Carolina to take advantage of the prevailing winds off the ocean.

From the chart, you can see that Langley was trying to make everything perfect. When something went wrong for the Wright brothers, they would say, "Oops, we crashed. Why did that happen? We think we crashed because of this and that. Okay, let's adjust the plane." The next day, they'd rebuild it and try something else. Then they'd crash again, take a guess at what caused it, make adjustments, and fly again the next day.

We take our time and find the levers, but like the Wright brothers, we move rapidly once we find them. That means we're going to start making a lot of mistakes fast. However, unlike so many business leaders, our definition of success is not "to get it right the first time."

Instead, our black boxes contain "success equals rapid reduction of practice." In other words, do it, learn the top two things you can, make an adjustment to your solution based on those top two things, and do it again as fast as you can with a deeper understanding of the key causes' and effects at play.

Forget getting it perfect the first time—whenever you learn something, you've been successful. The essence of our philosophy is rapidly learning, adjusting, and reducing a change to practice.

This approach can be very scary for leaders who are afraid to commit when they don't know if something will work. Instead of ready, aim, fire, their philosophy is to ready, aim, aim, aim, aim ... and then fire.

All that delay accomplishes is to slow everything down and produce fewer innovations per year. Demanding perfection the first time has another negative impact, too: it wastes man-hours by disempowering individual team members. If your team is charged with making changes, but anyone who makes a mistake will be held accountable, your team will likely involve many different people to displace risk and aim, aim, aim in the hopes that you won't fail.

The Wilbur and Orville Wright philosophy is to conduct thousands of little experiments in a year, knowing that success is defined by what you learn along the way. This philosophy means that you learn faster, make more progress in a year, and are more willing to take on seemingly impossible goals because you know there's no such thing as failure as long as you're learning.

You cannot predict all the unintended consequences as you innovate … you can only learn to rapidly discover them and make adjustments as you go forward.

This isn't about innovation training, tools, or techniques. It's about you, as a leader, changing the definition of success, setting "impossible" goals, and creating an environment in which your team can take risks to achieve them. That is how philosophy helps you gain traction for results.

The leader's role is to support the organization by creating an environment where the philosophy, principles, processes, and finally goals and metrics are clear. Instead of controlling or being a gatekeeper, the leader should be removing barriers, setting priorities, deploying resources, changing policies, and role modeling the new mindsets that will make the organization successful.

CHAPTER 9

TRACTION FOR RESULTS— PRINCIPLES

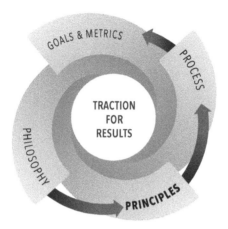

B efore we look at the principles component of the Traction for Results piece, let's take another look at the Depth of Thought and Action model.

DEPTH OF THOUGHT AND ACTION

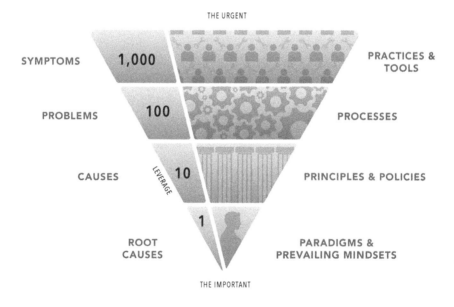

The component we just discussed—philosophy—is a part of the Paradigms and Prevailing Mindsets level at the bottom of the diagram, influencing everything else. The next level of the model, which is most directly influenced by the leader's philosophy, is principles and policies. Principles are a touchstone in the process of building an Enduring Organization.

GUIDING PRINCIPLES

We compiled the above list of principles over the years as we implemented key changes in numerous businesses. When we begin working with a new team, these are the principles that govern our approach. In the next section, we'll go into detail about each.

FOCUSING ON THE RIGHT "WHAT"

SEEK CLARITY

The first point in the "Focusing on the Right What" section is essential in the early stages of problem solving: seeking clarity. It's amazing how many leadership teams don't take the time to stop and seek clarity when they meet about what they're going to do. When we sit in on meetings and watch people work, they often say they're taking action on two or three different items, but they haven't agreed on what it is they're going to do. Usually, someone in the room who's short on patience will pipe up and say, "I'll just take care of it. Don't worry about it, you guys—I've got this one." And everyone else just agrees; Johnny's taking care of it, and it's one less thing they have to worry about. But what is Johnny really going to do? No one stops to ask for clarity.

A week later, the group will reconvene, and Johnny will present what he has done. Only then will the others realize that he was only talking about one action item, and several more were left adrift. Because no one in the group stopped to ask Johnny for more details, the whole team has just wasted a week

The problem is even more pronounced in teams that only meet once a month. If a group of top executives gets together to talk monthly, that's only 12 times up to the plate each year. Important decisions and course corrections need to be made, and you've only got 12 shots at it. Good luck; that doesn't work very well.

Seek clarity before agreeing to anything.

We teach our teams very quickly to seek clarity before agreeing to anything. Make sure you understand what your partner or teammates mean. Above all, make sure that whenever there's a commitment to take action, everybody's clear on what's actually going to happen.

It's very common for organizations to have a prevailing paradigm, primarily driven by the beliefs tucked away in the leaders' black boxes, that they organization has to do everything and fix every problem. But who has the time and resources to address everything? You don't.

That's why we use the 80/20 rule to focus on the levers—only work on the 20 percent of problems that will solve or greatly reduce 80 percent of the symptoms. Every time we visit a sales organization, we bring up the fact that approximately 20 percent of customers provide about 80 percent of sales. The sales team always insists it's more complicated than that, but the data inevitably backs us up.

It's also true in manufacturing. When we look at the data, we find that about 80 percent of the problems are caused by 20 percent of the issues. Say the company hasn't done its preventive maintenance, and the machines are down. When you look at the data, 78-84 percent of the downtime is caused by failure to perform preventative maintenance.

We always push the 80/20 rule because our goal isn't to fix everything—it's to find the biggest movers in the shortest period of time.

FACT-BASED DECISIONS

Have you ever been in a meeting where the group simply implemented the ideas of the most assertive person on the team or the most senior? Of course; we all have. But personality and even seniority aren't sufficient reason to put a plan into action.

Anything and everything your organization does should be based on good data.

There are prevailing myths about so many things in an organization; someone who's been with the company for 25 years will swear they're true. Nonetheless, we ask clients to humor us and let us do an analysis. When we bring in the data, people are often amazed at how many situations are completely different than what everyone thought.

More than half the time, the organization's direction is flawed because the appropriate level of analysis hasn't been done to get the facts. The result isn't necessarily erroneous data; often, it's just the misinterpretation of the numbers. With all the data resources available, it's important to choose the right ones, and use the right data when analyzing your current status or change efforts.

OUTCOMES VS. ACTIVITIES

The majority of an organization's language is framed in terms of activities rather than outcomes. For example, when they're addressing a problem, people often decide to hold a meeting to discuss an initiative.

But that's an activity. We want outcomes.

Instead of just holding a meeting, you need to be explicit about the purpose of the meeting and the outcomes you expect. For example, you need to ensure that you leave the meeting with an agreement on specific tasks and the deadlines for completing them, as well as who is responsible for each. That's the outcome.

"I'll call a meeting on that issue," and "I'll check with Susan and Paul on that" are activities, not outcomes. Outcomes sound like, "I'll hold a meeting by next Tuesday to interpret the data and produce a plan to implement the two or three key changes."

When leaders shift their thinking and language from activities to outcomes, their worlds starts to change. They have higher clarity about what they're doing, and things speed up so you get richer solutions faster.

If you have to produce an outcome by next Thursday, it doesn't matter if it takes one meeting or four—you have to do whatever it takes to get that outcome by that date.

Unfortunately, what often happens is that the scheduled meeting—the activity—takes place, but the meeting runs long and the issue goes unresolved. So, the group decides to hold another meeting a week later, and another after that, and the cycle continues without producing outcomes.

When organizations live for activities, things tend to drag on for too long. It takes far too much time to get anything done when the organization is not focused on outcomes.

THE TURNING POINT

MAKE A COMMITMENT, KEEP A COMMITMENT

The second category in our list of guiding principles is the turning point between Focusing on the Right "What" and How We Execute: Make a Commitment, Keep a Commitment.

Too often, teams just make excuses for not being able to follow through on their commitments. Maybe the meeting didn't take place because Johnny was on vacation, or something else came up: it's just another way of saying the dog ate your homework.

We teach people that before you place your name on the board next to an outcome due by a certain date, think about it. Because when you make a commitment, you need to *keep* that commitment. Without time-bound commitments, nothing much gets done in an organization.

One effective way to help team members keep their commitments is a classic: the buddy system. We often describe this concept as "two in a box" when we work with teams. When two people are paired up and really have each other's backs, they're more likely to keep their commitments, and things really get moving.

To be fair, sometimes delivering an outcome is a bigger job than originally thought. In cases like this, it's important to bring in whatever additional resources are needed to make a commitment possible. We want team members to swarm on a problem, get support from others, and use innovation to figure out how to keep the time commitment.

When you hold people to that principle, they can't go back to working by themselves; they have to ask for help, which is difficult for a lot of people to do. A lot of people prefer to work alone, so you need to push them to behave interdependently instead of independently. Working together outside of their comfort zones also teaches people to innovate.

BUILD YOUR PLAN BACKWARD FROM THE REQUIRED OUTCOME DATE.

The first of the guiding principles in the How to Execute section is to build your plan backward from the required outcome. To figure out what a project needs, get clear on the desired outcome and the deadline—for example, "We've got to have this done by May 15th"—and then work backward from that date.

LEARN AND ADJUST.

The 7X principle is one of our favorites, and we've used it in every project we've worked on in the more than 20 years that we've been doing this. When we go into an organization, the team will tell us that they're working on a given problem. We ask them what they've done to fix it, and they'll tell us about one or two attempts they made before they stopped trying.

The team may have good data and good analysis, but when their strategy doesn't work right away, they throw the problem in the "too hard" pile.

The 7X principle doesn't let people stop after one or two tries; instead, the early failures are opportunities to learn and adjust. If your team tried one solution and it didn't work, ask: What two things did we learn? What adjustment should we make tomorrow? That's the "learn and adjust" part.

Try, learn and adjust, and then try again. Each time, you get closer to a solution, and one or two tries simply don't get you close enough. We require that our teams try, learn, and adjust at least seven times, because we've already done our work finding the right "what" and making a commitment: now, it all comes down to perseverance.

Sometimes, teams will come back after three tries and report that something didn't work; we just hold up seven fingers, look at what they've learned, and send them off to adjust and try again. Before long, the 7X principle will become second nature.

MOVE QUICKLY

Throughout this book, we've exposed a number of activities that cause delay, such as the difference between activities and outcomes. However, we don't just want you to avoid delays; we want you to focus on moving quickly.

When creating change, developing a new product, or proving a concept, the most important thing you can do is rapidly turn your concept into something concrete, like a solution that can be tested. You want your ideas to become "real" as quickly as possible so that you and others can see and evaluate them, because testing enables you to move forward and learn the next step.

> The organization that learns
> and adjusts the fastest, wins.

The organization that learns the fastest, wins. Just like the Wright brothers, who rapidly conducted thousands of simple experiments while the Langley team was trying to get everything perfect for that one big flight, we learn and develop faster by doing, learning, and rapidly adjusting.

GO AND SEE.

Sometimes, when you're trying to solve a problem, you can sit and look at the data until your eyes cross, and facts and opinions begin to blur. That's when it's time to go and see the problem for yourself. Go to the plant floor, the nursing unit, or the lab and watch what's happening. That's the reality zone.

The map is not the country; you can stare at a map all day long, but when you visit the places on the map, it's a whole different experience. Likewise, when you go to the place where the real problems are, you start seeing things you never saw in the data alone. You can test your assumptions and start separating facts from fiction.

Toyota is particularly known for relying on the "go and see" principle. We've heard numerous stories of Toyota executives stopping meetings when conversations devolved into opinion and guesswork, and taking the whole team to the factory to go and see what was really happening.

Early in his career, Frank was asked to lead a chemical operation that was unable to meet the market's demand for a key product. Production in the facility had plateaued years earlier and had never improved. The company was missing out on millions of dollars in sales every year because it couldn't achieve a breakthrough.

In his new role, Frank walked past the dials in the plant's control room each day and noticed that the torque monitors showed a steady 17 percent for the machines that were the main constraint to his company's business. He'd been told many times that 17 percent was the absolute limit for those machines, and that many very bad things would happen if that number was ever exceeded.

However, staying at 17 percent meant that the company would continue to be stuck in its plateau and miss out on millions in revenue each year. This led Frank to wonder, why in the world would a machine designed to run safely and effectively at 120 percent torque be stuck at 17 percent? Enough was enough; it was time to find a way to safely test both the machine and the assumptions that were handcuffing the business.

As you might imagine, there were plenty of old, outdated assumptions and beliefs to overcome. Everyone in the plant was confident that they knew the limitations of the process. They all *knew* the magic number. Even the members of Frank's team were uneasy; it felt like the team was sailing toward the edge of the world. After so many years at 17 percent, opinion had become fact.

The time to "go and see" had arrived. A few minutes into the test, the machine approached 17 percent. All was well. Then, the dial was turned up and the torque abruptly rose to 19 percent. The massive machine rumbled for a few very long seconds and then quieted down. In that one moment, the company broke through its plateau and was running at higher outputs than at any time in its 15-year history.

As you might expect, 19 percent was just the beginning; by the end of the day, the team had demonstrated that the process could produce 4 times more than its prior record numbers. By going and seeing, the team wiped out the assumptions that were holding the business back and placed their company on a course to be the market leader.

BUT UNDER WHAT CONDITIONS COULD WE ACCOMPLISH THIS?

This guiding principle is how we respond when people are working toward a goal and decide it's impossible to reach.

We say, "I'm with you. Based on our current mindset and assumptions, it is impossible. But under what conditions could we accomplish this?"

This is a powerful question. It legitimizes the person who's stuck by agreeing with them that, as things currently stand, their task is impossible. Most people want to defend their positions, and by first legitimizing the person's concerns, you're helping him or her relax and let go of the mindset justifying why it can't change.

People can't innovate when they're busy defending their mindsets and protecting the contents of the black boxes. But, when you then ask under what conditions they *could* make it happen, you unlock a host of new ideas.

The sixth and final "how" from our guiding principles is "close the loop." If you're going to attempt a change, you first need to make sure there's a feedback loop in place.

What's the theory of improvement? Which metric should be measured? Where are the benefits showing up? It seems obvious, but when you make changes, follow up to see what happened. That's closing the loop. If there's an obvious gap after an action, then put in a process to close the loop.

These are the key principles to guide your teams by. Remember, you're in the execution mode. You're making your organization more capable and more responsive to your customers.

Sometimes, to create a loop and get sustainable results, you need to "Mr. Miyagi" your team.

If you've seen the 1984 movie *The Karate Kid*, you'll recall that the new kid in town, Daniel, gets picked on by the local big shots. He crosses paths with a gentleman—Mr. Miyagi—who turns out to be a karate master, and Mr. Miyagi decides to teach Daniel karate so he can protect himself from the bullies.

At first, Daniel is doing nothing more than painting a fence and sanding the floor. There are no karate lessons that we can see, yet all along Daniel is learning the mechanics of karate.

Every day, we drive our teams with the guiding principles in this chapter, and the natural byproduct is critical thinking, innovation, and great results.

Now it's time to learn about the third element in the Traction for Results anchor bolt: Process.

CHAPTER 10

TRACTION FOR RESULTS— PROCESS

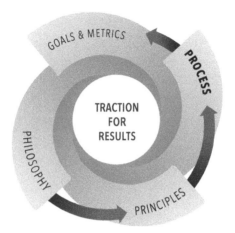

A few years ago, we were sitting in an auditorium with about 300 other people waiting for a workshop to begin. It was surprising that the speaker was doing any public speaking at all, let alone three-day workshops—he was 93 years old at the time.

Dr. W. Edwards Deming took the stage, his daughter pushing him in a wheelchair with an oxygen bottle strapped to the side. His opening remarks were delivered in a weak, raspy voice that we could barely understand, so everyone was leaning in to hear every word.

We sat in awe as he walked us through his philosophy, principles, and, of course, his process, which revolutionized the Japanese auto industry after being rejected initially by American automakers.

At 93, Dr. Deming was weak. He was able to stand only twice in those three days, and died within months of the workshop. He clearly was not doing it for the money or prestige.

He did it because he was honor-bound to live out his purpose: sharing how statistical process control can dramatically improve companies.

When he opened up the floor for questions, he more often than not answered with another question: "What process will you use to reach that objective?" We listened for three days and heard, "By what process?" three or four dozen times.

The process is how the organization intends to reach its goals.

We often find that leaders tackle our model backwards. They start with the Goals and Metrics component in the Traction for Results section of our model. They begin setting goals right away, but don't take the time to build a process supporting that change effort. They don't have a philosophy. There are no guiding principles. There are usually just mandates.

Pursuing goals without a process is a fool's errand.

For example, if you set a goal to improve your health, walking around the block three times after dinner might be sufficient. If your goal is to participate in a triathlon in six months, your process would be quite different.

A WORTHY GOAL

A big theme in implementation is the law of cause and effect. If you can't understand and influence cause and effect, you won't get the end result that you want: traction toward a new, relevant business model and results you can sustain.

The first piece of the process is to start with a worthy goal, one that will make your team members want to spend their energy on it and commit to it. This worthy goal can be framed as a problem that needs to be solved, or as an opportunity you want to take advantage of. If it's compelling enough, it'll make people think differently to achieve it.

Most businesses are under competitive pressure; either competitors offer products and services that the customer values and your organization doesn't offer, or competitors offer products that are of better quality or a lower price. That forces you to make some decisions, and many businesses make the same choice: cut costs.

Other goals are more aspirational or innovative, like an invention to fill a particular need.

Regardless, a goal designed to solve a problem has a tendency to deplete energy in an organization, while goal setting to take advantage of an opportunity tends to breathe energy into an organization. Either way, there's usually a portfolio of goals, whether framed as opportunities or as problems.

LEVERAGE IS AT THE INTERFACE

Another key concept in optimizing processes is that leverage occurs at points of interface.

For example, we visited a hospital lab that had gone from processing a blood sample in 45 minutes to performing the same function at the same level of quality in just 20 minutes. They were justifiably proud of themselves. However, they then sent the results to the patient's floor via fax, where they sat hidden among other department faxes for several hours.

Leverage occurs at points of interface.

The space between the laboratory and the nursing unit is an interface. Suppose the lab could do the test in two minutes; what does it matter if the results sit for hours in the busy nursing unit, unseen until after the patient's doctor completes his or her rounds? The doctor will have to wait until the next rounding cycle to act on the results, and the quality of care suffers—not to mention the length of the patient's stay.

The leverage in this case isn't how long the lab takes to process the sample, but the length of time between the lab and the doctor. We need to find a process that compresses the time between when the lab releases its results and when the doctor writes orders based on the lab's findings.

If you really want to make improvements, more often than not you need to look at the areas between departments. Usually, the baton is dropped when it's handed off, because no one is responsible for this "white space" between functions. In most organizations, job roles are designed to be responsible for a department or function. You need to set your goals to cover this "white space".

IDENTIFYING THE LEVERS

When you're pursuing results, it's important to understand the causal chain and to be able to identify the levers. As we discussed in depth in Chapter 7, levers are about understanding the critical few variables that make the difference in an organization. Not every ingredient in a recipe has the same power and weight; some are catalytic, like yeast, while others are not so impactful. Levers show us where we need to start.

Once you understand the levers and cause-and-effect relationships in your organization, you know where you can get the greatest gains with the least amount of resources. When a leader doesn't understand the idea of levers, the tendency is to attack 101 problems simultaneously at the symptom level, resulting in a game of whack-a-mole. We want to avoid that.

Companies that address symptoms as a way of life quickly become addicted to urgency. There's a lot of chaos, a lot of adrenalin, and a lot of blaming individuals for failing to solve problems at the process level. Just like a doctor resetting a broken bone for the good of the patient, the leader must reset the company by identifying levers, relentlessly implementing change, and ignoring the symptoms.

Dealing with the causal chain is where you become a scientist. How do things work? What happens in other parts of the company if I change this? Levers are like the pressure points in the body: Touch the right one in the right way, and you can heal damage or cause pain.

Business works the same way. It's about the "if–then"; *if* we move this key variable up into this range, *then* we can predict this kind of quality, cost, or throughput improvement.

You start with a goal, and then systematically lead your team through the process of identifying the critical few levers. Once you know those, you can understand the causes and effects of the key variables. Ask yourself, what has the greatest influence? List three to five things, and of those, choose the two with the biggest likelihood of impacting your results in a positive way. Work on those two "sub-levers" to start moving your levers.

Sometimes, you have the statistics you need right at your fingertips, and you can test a theory by looking at the data to determine where the change occurred. Often, you don't have the right measurement systems in place, but you can rapidly learn and adjust based on the experience of the team and test your theory within several days.

Say you've determined that you have two key levers, and you've also developed sub-levers. To move the two key levers, you need to achieve probably three or four specific outcomes, and you also need to make the whole operation time-bound by setting deadlines for outcomes.

In our experience, creating a planning document, or a road map, is very helpful for maintaining clarity and focus during this process.

Mission:

Goal:

Lever One

Lever Team	Sublevers	Who	2/1	2/8	2/15

Lever Two

Lever Team	Sublevers	Who	2/1	2/8	2/15

Road Map Template

For example, in the hospital case we referred to earlier, we determined that length of stay was impacting quality, costs, and profit. But length of stay was a challenging lever; how do you safely get a patient with pneumonia out of the hospital in three days when the hospital overage is five and a half days? Where would you start?

Using a road map like the template above, we determined the sub-levers that had the most influence on the big lever. We asked the experts, the doctors and nurses who dealt with issues every day, what was stopping patients from getting out on time?

They revealed a very powerful sub-lever: The doctors' rounds aren't in sync with results coming in from the ancillary departments. So Dr. Smith does rounds at 11:00 a.m., and visits the patient in room 314 at 11:26 a.m. A few of the tests that were ordered have come back, but the results don't make it into the patient's chart until after 1 p.m.

If that information had been available, Dr. Smith could have written new orders. Instead, it's the next day before the doctor sees the results. From this, you can see that one of the sub-levers affecting length of stay is the synchronization of the test results with the doctors' rounds. We added it to the road map.

When you're working on your roadmap, list the sub-levers that have the highest causal correlation or influence on the lever. And don't worry—at this point in the process, the majority of the items you come up with will feel impossible. That's good. It's a sign that you're very close to finding the differences that make a difference.

At this step in the process, you do not need to know how you will accomplish these things. All you need to do is list them. Just tell yourself and your team, "We'll figure out the *how* when the time comes." Then, apply the magic question: "It seems impossible with our current mindsets and assumptions, but under what conditions could we do this?"

METRICS TO SHOW PROGRESS

Your road map outlines your goal, the causal sub-levers, and the timeline—now you just need the right metrics to track your progress.

Metrics are the next component in the traction process. We'll delve more deeply into metrics in the next chapter, but they're also strongly linked to processes. Metrics tell you whether your new processes are working, and where you are in relation to your desired outcomes. Sometimes the right measurement systems already exist; other times they have to be built.

For instance, in our hospital project, we wanted to know how length of stay was measured. Every hospital in the country measures *average* length of stay, because they know they get paid against that.

What they don't have is a metric for how well the laboratories adhere to their timelines for delivering results. Nor do they measure when doctors make their rounds and how many reports are missed because of that timing. Those are both examples of metrics that we had to put in place.

You need a system that measures progress, or lack thereof, toward the goal. Most people don't even try to put those metrics in place; they just settle for some reports that are close to accurate. This is one area we usually need to address when we start working with an organization. It's not uncommon to be presented with 100 reports, only to find that maybe 20 of them are actually used by the team and have some value. The rest are just time-wasters for the people who have to spend hours crunching the numbers.

So the metrics need to be relevant, but how is that defined? In short, the most relevant measurement is the one that best characterizes progress toward your goal.

There are lots of ways to measure, and we don't pretend that all of the ones we use will be accurate right from the start. Many of our measurements are likely to change, because we'll get smarter about cause and effect and the nature of the real problem.

It's common for better metrics to be revealed as you implement solutions. We typically modify our measurement systems two or three times to make sure we're getting the clearest picture from the data; if the view through the lens is fuzzy, then you need to keep refocusing until you have clarity.

DAILY WORKOUTS

When we work with a client, we typically have what we call "workouts" twice a day. During these targeted meetings, we look at our road map and decide what outcomes have to be completed and what we need to do to ensure they get done.

In the "war room" where we meet, we have a commitment board to review the day-to-day commitments that will move the sub-levers and levers in the right direction. We post sticky notes on the wall to keep track of all that has yet to be achieved.

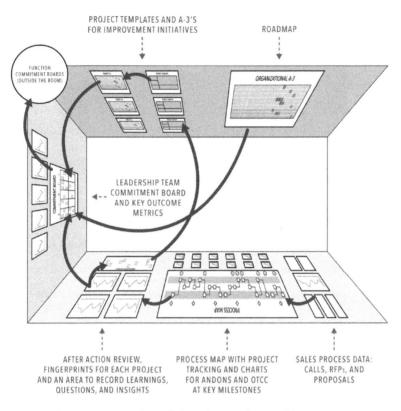

PROJECT TEMPLATES AND A-3'S
FOR IMPROVEMENT INITIATIVES

ROADMAP

FUNCTION
COMMITMENT BOARDS
(OUTSIDE THE ROOM)

ORGANIZATIONAL A-3

LEADERSHIP TEAM
COMMITMENT BOARD
AND KEY OUTCOME
METRICS

PROCESS MAP

AFTER ACTION REVIEW,
FINGERPRINTS FOR EACH PROJECT
AND AN AREA TO RECORD LEARNINGS,
QUESTIONS, AND INSIGHTS

PROCESS MAP WITH PROJECT
TRACKING AND CHARTS
FOR ANDONS AND OTCC
AT KEY MILESTONES

SALES PROCESS DATA:
CALLS, RFPs, AND
PROPOSALS

The war room makes all the relevant data visible, so you can
assess the status of the project in two minutes or less.

We use a three-by-five-foot sheet of paper labeled with each day of the work week, separated into morning and afternoon. Then, we determine what has to be done this morning, this afternoon, tomorrow morning, tomorrow afternoon, and so on.

Say we need to determine how long results sit in the nursing unit fax machine before they make it into the patient's chart. We need to put in a measurement system in place for that, and we've got to design it by tomorrow morning. Then, by tomorrow afternoon, we will have implemented our first data-gathering session.

All of those outcomes and deadlines would be included on our commitment board and posted in the war room, giving the leadership team clarity on what they have to do. Then, everyone has to report the findings back to the war room by a specific time so everyone can know what progress has been made.

Commitment Board

Due this week:

Monday	Tuesday	Wednesday	Thursday	Friday

Due next week:

Monday	Tuesday	Wednesday	Thursday	Friday

Each morning, we start marching through the outcomes on the commitment board. Which of them is linked up to a lever? Which of them caused a lever to move? As you begin to make progress on the levers, the profitability of the organization should improve.

Doing this twice a day is how we get traction. That's ten chances at bat each week, giving us a considerable edge on a competitor that's only problem-solving once a week or once a month. In two days, you can discover what takes your competition two months to figure out. It's hard to compete with a company that has such a tight execution process.

A month is too long to wait to find out if changes you're implementing have worked. How do you learn and adjust with that kind of time frame? You can't. So we install measurement systems and get daily results. If you see a change, great. If you don't, then you have to ask yourself an important question: Was it the right change and you just didn't execute it well, or was it the wrong change altogether?

Often, changes fail when they're first implemented, but it's not always the idea that was poor; it could have been the execution. It's important to distinguish between poor change and poor execution. That's why we require seven attempts at each change before giving up.

It's important to distinguish between poor change and poor execution.

The leader has a key role in each of these processes. You can't get traction on your change efforts without appropriate-minded leaders.

The leader's job is to provide support: removing obstacles, clarifying priorities, providing sufficient resources, changing policies, and role modeling new behaviors. The leader has to create the environment where these things happen naturally.

The result is traction: proof that the key metrics are moving in the right direction.

As we mentioned earlier, there are three process measures to watch—the Holy Grail. We want throughput to go up, quality to go up, and costs to go down. These will lead to the right outcome metrics, particularly increased profits.

The leader's role is to offer support, in order to enable the organization to get traction on the critical few levers. Now, let's look deeper at goal setting and metrics.

CHAPTER 11

TRACTION FOR RESULTS— GOALS & METRICS

N ow, at the very end of this book, we've finally reached the component that most leaders address first when they need to solve a problem.

Goal setting can be counter intuitive. Let us explain.

All too often leaders set goals and overlook the foundational elements that must be in place to reach those goals. If you start with setting the goal, then cycle down to the bottom of The Enduring Leadership model to Relevant Business Model, then Appropriate Minded Leaders, Insightful Organizations and Traction for Results.

We purposely designed the model to start with the often over looked elements to ensure they do not get lost in the urgency of solving problems.

The business model is in place, appropriate-minded leaders are on board, the organization has cultivated insight, and the team is gaining traction as it executes change efforts.

Here, then, is where we set our goals and define our standards for measuring those goals.

THE GOALS

There are several philosophies on goal setting.

Some leaders believe that you don't set a goal, you pursue perfection. You just do the best you can, and you keep getting better and better. Because if somebody says, "Let's set a goal of 10 percent," you'll probably get to 10 percent, but then everyone stops trying.

There are also leaders who subscribe to the philosophy that you've got to set goals that are reachable, say, for 10 or 20 percent improvement. We aren't big fans of these goals, because what often happens is that people try to reach them by doing the same things harder and faster. This may help them reach the goal, but it leads to change that isn't sustainable. People are just trimming fat or achieving change through a dash of heroics, but no one's really updating the contents of their black boxes. They're not changing their fundamental assumptions.

Instead, we like to set goals that seem impossible—and the first thing everyone does is laugh. "That's ridiculous," they'll say. But these goals quickly push them to a place where they have to think fundamentally differently to make progress; they can't just do what they've been doing harder and faster. They've got to innovate to find a different way of doing things.

Yes, we set significant goals, but we also back them up with processes to achieve them.

Here's our goal-setting philosophy:

If something requires a month to do, we reduce that time to one week. If something takes a week to do, we cut that to one day. Things that take about a day must be done in an hour, and anything that takes an hour must be completed in a minute.

"Compelling goals automatically push you to look for solutions in a different space."

Such compelling goals automatically push you to look for solutions in a different space, which in turn makes you more likely to stay ahead of the competition.

In this particular instance, we want people to think in terms of minutes instead of hours. This is one way we introduce innovation into the equation. Simply getting people talking and thinking in a completely different unit of measure changes the game.

Simply getting people talking and thinking in a completely different unit of measure changes the game.

When you set big goals, you must have a process behind them. As we discussed in the last chapter, when approaching any goal, you must ask yourself, "What process will I use to achieve that?" Likewise, process is sharpened by principles, and principles flow from philosophy.

Each element of the Enduring Organization Leadership Model builds on the last, leading up to Goals and Metrics. By the time you reach the goal-setting stage, you have built a solid foundation for an Enduring Organization.

In summary, set goals at a level that makes it impossible for people to think the way they've been thinking, but be sure to couple those goals with a process—that's what gives your team the space to rapidly innovate, learn, and adjust.

The people we work with tend to get excited about this approach to goal setting. Instead of having 99 problems to solve, they just need to focus on two or three. Once they've learned this new skill, they can apply it to other areas of the organization.

After we leave our engagement, the team doesn't stop behaving this way. They're still thinking in outcomes. They're still making commitments and keeping them. They're still trying seven times to make a change without giving up.

THE METRICS

The right goals are essential, but if you don't have good metrics, you're flying blind. Just think about a pilot that doesn't trust his instruments; he'd be in a bit of trouble. Or what about a doctor doing robotic surgery—if the camera is misaligned or the lens is distorted, she'll cut and suture in the wrong place.

You've got to be able to see what's really going on; that's where metrics come in. But more often than not, the metrics an organization is using are flawed. One common reason is that the operational definitions aren't very good. You can't have a measurement system without first seeking clarity on the operational definitions of the variables you're measuring.

For example, say we need to start a timer at the beginning of a run on the production line. It makes a big difference if one person's operational definition of "beginning of the run" is when the button is pushed, while another person thinks it means when the machine has warmed up and is running at the standard rate.

A measurement system can also be flawed by *how* data is collected. Some people record metrics in real time, which is what we want, but others just approximate their metrics. They'll record their approximate start and stop times at the end of a shift just because it's required, and at that point, they're relying on memory. If you're batching measures at the end of the day instead of reporting in real time, expect to have inaccurate and incomplete data. Real-time metrics are the basis of an effective measurement system.

Flawed or not, most metrics have a tendency to measure only a certain function or department—they measure things vertically. How well does this silo do this particular thing? The real value in an organization flows across functions; it happens horizontally rather than vertically, and the measurement system must be aligned with the flow of the value that's being created.

You need a metric that measures across a function as it flows through the organization. These are rare, but without them your organization is flying blind. Without being able to measure across a function, you can't accurately determine how long it takes to do a particular activity, or to what degree of quality the activity was performed. Without this information, it's difficult to tell how broken an organization is. Worse still, if you don't trust your measurement system, how will you know that a change you implemented is performing correctly?

More often than not, we have to install a measurement system ourselves and create common operational definitions that show the flow of value across the business.

When you're working to gain traction for results, you'd better have a good philosophy, you'd better consistently act with good principles of execution and innovation, you'd better set compelling goals and couple those with processes for making change, and you need to have good metrics in place or you won't know whether your changes are working.

The big takeaway here is that you should never set big, compelling goals on a tight timeline without processes in place to achieve the goal and flow metrics to measure it. That's just unfair to your team.

TRAIL MAGIC

Every few years, Hal and about eight of his old college buddies go out to a 5,000-acre working ranch in Wyoming to spend a week riding horses in the mountains.

One day, Hal and two or three of his friends decided to take a day-long trail ride up to the top of a nearby mountain. They rode for about four hours to reach the summit, and enjoyed the stillness of being miles and miles from any other living soul.

It had been a gorgeous day when they started, but when they were about two-thirds of the way up, the sky began to darken. By the time they reached the top, a storm was rolling in and they were a three or four hour ride from shelter. The clouds moved in around them, and visibility quickly dropped. The trail markings were no longer visible, and tension was beginning to mount.

Then, out of the clouds walked a solitary hunter carrying a bow and arrow, no more than 20 yards away. They hadn't been expecting to see a soul so far into the mountains, and he seemed like an apparition.

The man greeted the group and explained that he'd been in the mountains hunting elk for two weeks. After some conversation, they asked him if he happened to know where the trailhead was. "Sure!" he said, giving them careful directions. Then he walked away, and the clouds swallowed him up just as quickly as he had appeared.

After returning home, Hal told his son Pete this story. "That was trail magic!" Pete said, and explained that when you put yourself at risk and go outside of your comfort zone, special things can happen.

The same is true in business. When you set really compelling goals and take bold risks, the universe has a tendency to provide you with what you need.

MALCOLM'S TRAIL MAGIC

Years ago, we were working on an emergency project in which we had to improve capacity by 30 percent in 60 days, at a plant that was operating at maximum capacity. It was a very big goal to accomplish in a very short period of time, so we decided to review the literature to see if anyone in a non-competing industry had been successful with the strategies we were considering.

Lo and behold, we found a similar organization in a different industry that had made some exciting breakthroughs, and we wondered if any of the innovations would translate over. We were behind on this project and struggling to meet the target date.

We called the owner of the business, a 70-year-old gentleman named Malcolm. When we told him about our problem, he not only offered us a solution—he sent two of his best people to spend a week with us to show us how to implement his innovations. Malcolm was not only willing to give up his secrets; he was willing to use his company's resources, the foremen, to help us use them. That's also trail magic.

When you set really compelling goals, you're forced to get vulnerable and start thinking in different ways. Ideas come to you. You begin to see that the answers you need are not only outside of your expertise, but beyond the limits of your old, outdated assumptions. Sometimes, you've just got to empty your black box and start over.

AFTERWORD

Throughout this book, we've described our Enduring Organization Leadership Model as a counterclockwise process beginning with a Relevant Business Model, moving on to Appropriated-Minded Leaders, and then Insightful Organizations, ending with Traction for Results.

It's clearly not linear in any way, yet the sequence does follow a logical pattern. The four elements are interdependent, and should be treated as such. When environmental realities make it necessary for you to upgrade your business model, your success is dependent on the fundamental assumptions of your organization's leadership team. The mindsets of the leaders define the organization's capability to implement the new business model, because they influence the team's ability to execute the critical changes at a faster rate than ever before. Before you make a change in one of the four elements, ask yourself what the implications are for the others.

This model can be used to test your company's potential to become and remain an Enduring Organization. If you're particularly challenged in one area, use the model to check and see if the four elements of that anchor bolt are in place.

If you've been working hard on improvement efforts for years but can't gain ground fast enough, it's time to take a good hard look at the health of your anchor bolts.

SUFFICIENT INTENT

At the end of the day, becoming and remaining a relevant organization comes down to one thing—sufficient intent.

"Whether you think you can, or you think you can't—you're right."

—HENRY FORD

Whether it's the Wright Brothers first flight, Ernest Shackleton's voyage to the Antarctic, or your journey to become and remain an Enduring Organization, success all boils down to sufficient intent.

Leaders need to ...

❋ *Refresh* their business models to keep their organizations relevant.

* *Breathe* in new, appropriate beliefs and mindsets and ensure that their organizations have leaders who are willing and able to implement the relevant business model.

* *See* their organizations for what they really are and foster company cultures in which all team members can have and share insights into how the company operates.

* *Support* high-leverage changes and provide traction with ideas and processes to achieve key results.

This journey cannot be delegated. Leadership at all levels must be fully committed.

Whether you find your organization approaching a rolling-over business model or a need to step up your ongoing performance improvement processes, our intention is for the Enduring Leadership model to be an aid for support on your journey.

Becoming and remaining an Enduring Organization will be a most difficult and rewarding achievement. There is no easy button to hit or shortcuts to take, but when achieved, it will be one of the most fulfilling experiences of your career.

Thank you for the gift you gave us by giving up your time to read our book. These concepts have helped organizations reach seemingly unreachable goals, and we fully expect them to help you and your organization as well.

Godspeed on your journey.

Hal McLean
Frank Mellon

ABOUT THE AUTHORS

ABOUT HAL

In his twenty-five years of managing The McLean Group, Hal McLean has honed a unique ability to liberate hidden capacity in businesses, creating value far beyond the bottom line.

Major companies often call on Hal after larger consulting firms have tried and failed to create the fundamental changes that are needed. Hal's knack for tackling big, complex problems in new ways helps him deliver impressive results, often without any additional capital.

As a recent college graduate, Hal began working with the Fortune 500 company Owens Corning. He rapidly became one of the company's most successful salesmen and was fast-tracked for promotion, rising quickly through the company. Within a few years, he found himself working as a business analyst under the vice president of the company's three largest divisions.

It was in this role that Hal discovered his aptitude for cutting through the noise to identify the "levers" in each business that lead to significant performance improvements. In his own words, he learned to find "the difference that makes the difference."

After ten years with Owens Corning, Hal moved to Wilson Learning to develop his skills in managing corporate change. Five years later, he founded The McLean Group to take his skills to new heights. When he started the business, Hal and his wife Barb already had two children. She wisely told him, "Go for it, you can always find another job." As it turned out, she had nothing to worry about.

Today, Hal and Barb live in lovely Knoxville, Tennessee. They have three adult children—Jenn, Molly, and Pete—all of whom currently manage their own businesses.

ABOUT FRANK

In a nearly thirty-year career innovating in Fortune 500 companies and his own business, Mellon Solutions, Frank Mellon has built a reputation for identifying and capturing value for clients on an exceptional scale. His flair for recognizing untapped opportunity and putting it to work has created significant bottom-line impact for his clients, often at levels they've not imagined.

He has been working with The McLean Group since Frank founded his consulting company, Mellon Solutions, in 2002. In fact, Hal was Frank's first client, and they've been working together ever since.

Whether designing and implementing strategy with executives or working with front-line teams discovering breakthroughs to double their outputs, the recurring theme in Frank's work is "move the levers that drive change and create lasting value for the client."

Clients see Frank not only as an expert at identifying the levers that can elevate their businesses but also as a leader and advisor they can rely on to help guide and accelerate their efforts to create lasting change.

Difficult, long-standing problems are usually the ones that slow a company's progress. Frank helps businesses take those on and reinvent themselves with a fact-based approach that builds clear strategies and measurements that are simple to execute.

Frank lives in Elizabethtown, Kentucky, with Jacque. He and Jacque love going golfing with their son and, whenever possible, spending time with their brand-new grandson, Jake.

OUR OFFERINGS

THE MCLEAN GROUP AND MELLON SOLUTIONS OFFER:

On-site executive sessions

Organization assessments

Performance-improvement projects

Pre-sale value enhancement

The McLean Group, Inc.
the-mclean-group.com

Mellon Solutions
mellon-solutions.com

Printed in the USA
CPSIA information can be obtained
at www.ICGtesting.com
JSHW072028140824
68134JS00044B/3827